THE

TASTY RECIPES TO
SET YOU UP FOR LIFE

INDEPENDENT
COOK

SARAH MAIN

In memory of

my Mum, who was an inspirational lady, lived life to
the full and was a great cook
and
my Dad, who loved food and to whom I promised I
would write a cookbook one day.

THE

TASTY RECIPES TO SET YOU UP FOR LIFE

INDEPENDENT

SARAH MAIN

COOK

Photography by Christine Bradshaw

BATSFORD

CONTENTS

DESSERTS

BAKING

BASICS

INTRODUCTION

The Independent Cook is comprised of fail-safe recipes that hundreds of people have tested over the years. All of them can be prepared, cooked (and most of the washing up done) within one hour.

I have been a Food Technology teacher for over 30 years, and this book is the result of collating, refining and perfecting recipes. I've wanted to write a cookbook ever since I left my first teaching stint to raise a family, but didn't have the time to kickstart things until COVID hit in 2020. Despite that, I had been subconsciously working on the book for many years prior to actually sitting down and starting to type – through teaching, learning practically and helping my own children with their kitchen adventures. In doing the latter, I have also learned first-hand what is really useful to have in terms of basic equipment, so I have made a list in case you are just starting your cooking journey. The list of essential equipment (see page 14) includes everything you will need if you want to be able to make every recipe in the book. I've also included a list of optional extra equipment needed for some recipes (although there is usually an alternative), a glossary of terms at the back of the book (see page 184) and a conversion chart for temperatures and measurements. I also wanted to ensure that the book has a clear photo for each dish – personally, I like to know what I am aiming for when cooking from a recipe book!

During a break in lockdown, I met up with Christine Bradshaw, who very kindly offered to take the photos for the book. At first it was difficult because of COVID – at the start I would drop food off on her doorstep wearing a face mask and then go home to discuss everything over Zoom. There was so much to consider that I had never given any thought to before: props, lighting, mood, texture, background, surfaces… The list goes on. Thankfully, when restrictions were lifted, we were able to meet up in person and the conversations became easier and more familiar. We talked about how to accomplish each photo and then borrowed fabric, dishes, cutlery and lots more from various people to achieve our goal. Seeing the finished photographs each time gave me enormous gratification, and kept the book going as we progressed.

I have been an avid cook ever since I was a young girl. One of my earliest memories of cooking is helping my Nan and Grandad to prepare and serve home-grown produce. I used to sit and string, chop and blanch runner beans in their garden during the height of the season, then portion them out and put them into the freezer. My Nan would also bottle jars and jars of excess tomatoes, and their love of gardening and maximising their produce has certainly been passed down to me. I have a relatively small garden, but I thoroughly enjoy the satisfaction of growing something from seed and being able to incorporate it into my cooking using the final product.

I made my first 3-tiered wedding cake at the age of 13, started cooking a meal once a week on a budget for myself and my Mum, and then went to catering college to complete a diploma in Hotel and Catering Management. After that, I completed a work placement at the Savoy in the pastry section (the carrot cake on page 138 is an adapted recipe that I used there), before travelling around Australia, working in the restaurant industry either as a chef or front of house. I subsequently returned to England to complete a 4-year BEd Hons degree in teaching Technology (Food, Textiles and Design Technology). Since then, I have taught mainly Food and Textiles.

I have always been passionate about food and have been lucky enough to visit many fantastic restaurants around the world (and some not so lovely!), collecting inspiration and ideas along the way. I hope that, for you, *The Independent Cook* sparks your own journey with food.

Sarah x

USING THE RECIPES

THE SYMBOLS

At the top of each recipe, there will be a combination of various symbols (outlined below). These should hopefully make it easier to work out which recipe is best for you, for example with the equipment you have, at a quick glance.

Basic equipment list This is what is required if you want to make every recipe in the book!

Extra equipment A list on each recipe will flag any extra equipment required, if necessary. This usually refers to a gadget that will make life easier, but often there is an alternative.

Quantity Each recipe will tell you how many people it will serve or the number it makes, if individual items such as cookies. This is an average and will depend on your portioning.

QR codes Some recipes contain a QR code linking to a video. These videos are straightforward demonstrations of how to do an element of the recipe. For easy reference, there is a list of all the QR codes on pages 182–183.

Freezing quantities are relatively small for most recipes as most people need to cook on a budget, although you can double up most recipes and freeze half. There will be a symbol at the top of the recipe which will tell you if it is suitable for freezing. If it is, it can be frozen for up to 3 months (or up to 1 month if containing meat or fish) as a general rule. When reheating, only reheat once and make sure it is piping hot.

NOTES ON RECIPES

Vegetarian Most recipes that contain meat can be made vegetarian with meat substitutes.

Oil If the recipe says oil, then sunflower or vegetable oil is best to use here. Olive oil would be too strong a flavour to use for these recipes. This is usually for greasing a tin or baking tray.

Serving suggestions These are included with most of the recipes to give you an idea of how to serve each dish. Often this will include ingredients that are not in the main recipe, such as condiments. These optional serving suggestions can be found highlighted in a coloured circle and are just there to provide some inspiration – you can serve the dishes however you like!

Tips Most of the recipes include a tip which can be found at the bottom of the recipe. This is there to give you options for adaptations with ingredients or equipment, guidance with certain methods, or healthier alternatives (for example).

BEFORE STARTING TO COOK

- Wash your hands
- Put your apron on
- If you have long hair, tie it back
- Read the recipe all the way through
- Check you have all the ingredients and equipment

Before you begin cooking any recipe, it is always good practice to follow a few strict guidelines, in order to keep you and anyone you might be cooking for safe and avoid food poisoning.

You should always wash your hands thoroughly with warm, soapy water before handling any ingredients. It is also a good idea to put an apron on, to keep harmful bacteria from your clothes getting onto food as well as to keep your clothes clean while you work. If your hair is long, tie it back so that you don't end up with any unwanted 'extra ingredients' in your dish. It is also safer as it will prevent it catching fire or getting tangled in machinery!

Always have a high level of food hygiene standards: make sure that you wash your hands after touching any raw meat, fish and eggs, and do the same with any equipment that it touches (such as knives or chopping boards). While teaching, I always use the paint analogy with my students – I pretend the raw meat or fish is covered in red paint that spreads to whatever it comes into contact with. This helps visualise how potentially harmful bacteria can do the same.

Remember to cover/wrap everything that's placed in the fridge and keep raw meat and raw fish at the bottom of the fridge to prevent cross contamination.

You should also make sure to wash any vegetables you are going to be using before you prepare them.

BASIC STORE CUPBOARD

Baking parchment (or greaseproof paper)
Cling film (plastic wrap)
J-cloth (dish cloth)
Muffin cases
Olive oil/vegetable oil
Oven gloves (oven mitts)
Pepper
Plain (all-purpose) flour
Salt
Sugar
Tea towel (dish towel)

ESSENTIAL EQUIPMENT

- Baking tray
- Cake tin (20cm/8 inch round)
- Can opener
- Chopping board
- Fish slice (flipper)
- Fork (metal)
- Frying pan
- Grater
- Kettle
- Knife – bread/serrated
- Knife – butter
- Knife – large (chopping)
- Knife – small (paring)
- Measuring jug (in millilitres/fl oz)
- Measuring spoon set
- Mixing bowl
- Muffin tin
- Mug
- Pastry brush
- Peeler
- Rectangular roasting tin (about 26cm x 20cm x 4cm/ 10½ x 8 x 1½ inch)
- Rectangular roasting tin (about 34cm x 24cm x 4cm/ 13½ x 9½ x 1½ inch)
- Rolling pin
- Saucepan – large, with lid
- Saucepan – small
- Scales
- Scissors
- Sieve/Colander
- Spatula
- Spoons in various sizes
- Tongs
- Whisk (balloon or electric hand mixer)
- Wire rack/cooling rack
- Wooden spoon

OPTIONAL EXTRA EQUIPMENT

For some recipes you may need some of the following equipment – if so, it will be clearly marked at the top of the recipe. Alternatives are in italics.

- Lemon squeezer (*you can use your hand and squeeze over a bowl*)
- Hand stick blender
- Electric hand whisk
- Food processor
- Garlic crusher (*or chop it finely on a board*)
- Tongs (*two forks will do*)
- Skewers (*for Kebabs, on page 80*)
- Wok (*a large frying pan can be used instead*)
- Potato masher (*a fork can be used instead but it won't be quite as smooth as with a masher*)
- Ovenproof dish (*or use a small rectangular roasting tin, for example for Shepherd's Pie on page 70, or Fruit Crumble on page 116*)
- Loaf tin (about 20 x 10 x 6cm/8 x 4 x 2½ inch)
- Round biscuit cutters (*or you can cut shapes out with a knife*)
- Palette knife (*a fish slice or butter knife will do*)
- Sushi rolling mat (*or use a sheet of foil covered in cling film/ plastic wrap*)
- 4-hole Yorkshire pudding tray (*for Toad in the Hole on page 110 – a small roasting tin can be used instead*)

SOUPS

4 Serves 4

 Suitable for freezing

 Hand stick blender

 Saucepan with lid

HOW TO:

MAKING
CROUTONS

INGREDIENTS

1 small onion

1 tablespoon olive oil

1 teaspoon cumin seeds or
ground cumin

Pinch of chilli flakes or chilli
powder

6 medium carrots (650g/
1lb 7oz)

2 teaspoons sugar

700ml (24fl oz) vegetable/
chicken stock

½ bunch of coriander
(cilantro)

Salt and pepper

4 tablespoons crème fraîche
(optional)

For the croutons (optional)

2 slices bread

1 tablespoon oil

CARROT & CORIANDER SOUP

METHOD

1   Peel and chop the onion into small pieces.

2   Put the oil into a saucepan on a medium heat and add the onion, frying and stirring it until it softens (this will take about 3 minutes).

3   Add the cumin and the chilli and cook for 30 seconds.

4   Peel and chop the carrots into rough pieces. Add the carrots, sugar and stock to the saucepan and bring it to the boil. Once boiling, turn down to a low heat and simmer with the saucepan lid on for 15 minutes, or until the carrot is very soft, then remove from the heat.

5   Add the coriander and, using a hand stick blender, carefully (as it will be very hot) blend the soup until smooth. Add a splash of water if it is too thick.

6   Add salt and pepper to taste.

7   Swirl the crème fraîche through the soup with a spoon, if using.

8   If making croutons, cut the bread into 1cm (½ inch) cubes. Heat the oil in a frying pan on a high heat, add the bread cubes and fry them, turning them constantly, until golden and crispy.

9   Serve with the croutons, if using, or wholemeal crusty bread rolls.

Photographed with croutons and a sprinkling of coriander

4 Serves 4

 Suitable for freezing

 Hand stick blender

HOW TO:

SKINNING
TOMATOES

TOMATO SOUP

INGREDIENTS

1kg (2lb 2oz) tomatoes (plum tomatoes work well)

2 tablespoons oil

1 onion

1 carrot

1 celery stalk

2 tablespoons tomato purée (tomato paste)

1 vegetable/chicken stock cube dissolved in 500ml (17fl oz) boiling water

20g (¾oz) fresh basil leaves (optional)

Salt and pepper

4 tablespoons single (light) cream, to serve (optional)

To make cream of tomato soup, pour the soup into bowls and stir through the cream, or drizzle the cream on the top of each bowl.

METHOD

1   Carefully make a cross on the base of the tomatoes, just cutting through the skin with a sharp knife. Place them in a mixing bowl and cover with boiling water for 1 minute. You should see the skin starting to peel away from the tomatoes (if it doesn't, leave them for another minute). Drain the water using a sieve or colander and carefully peel the tomatoes, discarding the skins. Chop the tomatoes into quarters.

2   Put the oil in a large saucepan. Peel and chop the onion and carrot into small pieces. Chop the celery into small pieces and add them to the saucepan.

3   Fry the vegetables on a medium heat for 3–5 minutes until they start to soften.

4   Add the tomatoes, tomato purée and stock and bring to the boil. Once boiling, turn down the heat and simmer for 20 minutes with the lid on.

5   Take off the heat and add the basil, if using. With a hand stick blender, carefully (as it will be very hot) blend the soup until it is smooth.

6   Season to taste with salt and pepper.

 You can spice this up with a pinch of chilli powder.

20   SOUPS

Photographed with a drizzle of cream

4 Serves 4

 Suitable for freezing

 Saucepan with lid

Serve with grated Parmesan or Cheddar cheese on top.

INGREDIENTS

1 large carrot

1 small onion

2 sticks celery

1 potato

1 garlic clove

1 tablespoon oil

1 tablespoon tomato purée (tomato paste)

1 vegetable stock cube dissolved in 400ml (14fl oz) boiling water

200g (7oz) canned chopped tomatoes

1 teaspoon dried oregano (optional)

70g (2½oz) small pasta (I recommend conchigliette/small shells)

50g (1¾oz) green beans

Salt and pepper

4 teaspoons grated Parmesan or Cheddar cheese

MINESTRONE SOUP

METHOD

1 Prepare the carrots, onion, celery and potato by peeling and chopping them into even-sized pieces – approximately 2cm (¾ inch) chunks or slices – as you will see them in the soup. Finely chop or crush the garlic clove.

2 Heat the oil in a saucepan on a medium heat and add the chopped vegetables. Cook for 5 minutes until they have softened slightly, stirring occasionally.

3 Stir in the tomato purée, stock, tomatoes and oregano. Bring the soup to the boil, then lower the heat and simmer with the lid on for 5 minutes.

4 Add the pasta and stir in. Cook the soup for a further 5 minutes.

5 Wash the green beans and cut the ends off, then cut into 2cm (¾ inch) long pieces. Add the beans and stir in. Cook for a final 5 minutes.

6 Season to taste with salt and pepper.

 You can add other vegetables and white beans to this soup and leave out any vegetables that you don't like.

Photographed with a topping of grated Parmesan cheese

2 Serves 2

 Suitable for freezing

 Hand stick blender

Pour the soup into bowls and swirl through the crème fraîche, if using. You can also garnish with pea shoots and mint leaves.

PEA & MINT SOUP

INGREDIENTS

1 large potato

700ml (24fl oz) stock (can be made with a stock cube and boiling water)

1 garlic clove

4 spring onions (scallions)

300g (10½oz) frozen peas

3 stalks fresh mint

Salt and pepper

2 tablespoons crème fraîche (optional)

Pea shoots and mint leaves, to garnish (optional)

METHOD

1 Peel the potato and chop into very small pieces, then put them into a saucepan with the stock.

2 Peel and chop or crush the garlic and add it to the pan.

3 Wash and chop the spring onions into small pieces, discarding the root, then add them to the pan. Bring the liquid to the boil, then simmer for 15 minutes.

4 Add the peas to the saucepan and simmer for a further 5 minutes.

5 Pick the mint leaves off their stalks and chop roughly.

6 Take the soup off the heat and add the mint.

7 Using a hand stick blender, carefully (as it will be very hot) blend the soup until it is smooth.

8 Season to taste with salt and pepper.

 If you haven't got a hand stick blender, you can leave the soup chunky.

Photographed with pea shoots and mint leaves

Serves 4

 Hand stick blender

Enjoy it with fresh, crusty ciabatta, baguette or toasted sourdough bread.

INGREDIENTS

500g (1lb 2oz) large, ripe tomatoes

2 (bell) peppers (any colour)

½ cucumber

2 spring onions (scallions), or ½ red onion

1 garlic clove

4 tablespoons olive oil

2 tablespoons red wine vinegar

Juice of ½ lemon

1 teaspoon sugar

Salt and pepper

GAZPACHO

METHOD

1 Chop the tomatoes roughly. Remove the stalks from the peppers, then deseed and chop them up roughly. Peel the cucumber and cut it up roughly. Trim the ends of the spring onions and cut up finely. (You can save a tablespoon of these chopped ingredients for garnish if you want to.)

2 Peel and chop the garlic, then put it into a large mixing bowl with the tomatoes, peppers, cucumber and spring onions.

3 Add the oil, vinegar, lemon juice and sugar.

4 Blend it with a hand stick blender until smooth.

5 Put the soup in the fridge for at least 2 hours (and up to 24 hours) until it is really cold.

6 Add salt and pepper to taste.

7 Serve chilled, garnished with a leftover tablespoon of chopped vegetables.

 This is a delicious cold soup that is generally eaten in the summer.

Photographed with chopped spring onion and toasted sourdough bread

SNACKS
& SIDES

GUACAMOLE

HOW TO:

HALVE AND
STONE AN
AVOCADO

INGREDIENTS

1 large ripe tomato

1 lime

3 ripe avocados

1 small red onion

1 chilli (red or green)

Salt and pepper

Handful of coriander
(cilantro)

Serve with
tortilla chips, or
it makes a great
accompaniment to
fajitas (page 76).

METHOD

1 Finely chop the tomato on a chopping board, then tip it into a mixing bowl.

2 Squeeze the lime to extract as much juice as possible.

3 Carefully halve the avocados and remove the stones, then use a spoon to scoop out the flesh. Cut it into rough 1cm (½ inch) cubes, then add to the bowl with the tomato.

4 Pour the lime juice over the avocado to prevent it from going brown.

5 Peel and finely chop the onion and add it to the bowl.

6 Deseed the chilli, chop it into tiny pieces and add it to the mixing bowl. (Do not touch your eyes when doing this and make sure you wash your hands thoroughly once you have finished chopping the chilli.)

7 Mix it all together and add a pinch of salt and pepper to taste. If you prefer it less chunky, either mash it with a fork or put it in a blender or food processor and blitz it a little using the pulse button.

8 Chop the coriander and scatter it over the guacamole.

 If you're not serving straight away, cover the dip with cling film (plastic wrap) and chill until needed.

TZATZIKI

Serve as a dip with warm pitta bread or carrot sticks, or as an accompaniment to barbecue food!

METHOD

1 Put the yoghurt into a small bowl.

2 Wash the cucumber and cut it in half lengthways. Scoop out the seeds with a teaspoon, then chop it into small pieces and add it to the yoghurt.

3 Peel and crush the garlic and add it to the bowl.

4 Take the mint leaves off the stalk and chop the leaves finely – discard the stalks. Add the chopped mint to the mixture and stir it gently with a metal spoon.

5 Season to taste with salt and pepper.

6 The dip will keep in the fridge for up to 3 days.

INGREDIENTS

200g (7oz) natural Greek yoghurt

½ cucumber

1 garlic clove

3 sprigs of mint

Salt and pepper

4 Serves 4

 Food processor

Serve the dip with a sprinkling of pomegranate seeds and a drizzle of olive oil (as in the picture).

INGREDIENTS

1 x 400g (14oz) can of chickpeas

1 garlic clove

1 lemon

5 tablespoons olive oil, plus extra if needed

½ teaspoon ground cumin

½ teaspoon paprika

2 tablespoons tahini

Salt and pepper

HUMMUS

METHOD

1　Pour the chickpeas into a sieve and rinse them with cold water. Save 1 tablespoon of whole chickpeas to garnish the hummus. Put the rest into a food processor.

2　Peel and crush (or finely chop) the garlic and add to the chickpeas in the food processor.

3　Squeeze the juice from the lemon and add it to the food processor.

4　Add the remaining ingredients (except the saved whole chickpeas) and blend together. Keep adding extra oil, a tablespoon at a time, if needed, until you get a smooth paste. You may need to pause the food processor several times and scrape down the sides of the bowl using a spatula or spoon.

5　Taste and add a pinch of salt and pepper if needed.

6　Tip the hummus into a bowl and garnish it with the saved whole chickpeas.

7　The dip will keep in the fridge for up to 3 days.

 You can add extra ingredients to the food processor such as roasted red peppers. It is delicious with hot pitta bread or thin sticks of carrot, cucumber and celery for dipping.

4 Serves 4

 Food processor

Ideal as a dip served with tortilla chips or pitta bread, or as an accompaniment to fajitas (page 76).

INGREDIENTS

200g (7oz) cherry tomatoes

1 garlic clove

½ red onion

1 green or red chilli

1 x jar of roasted red peppers (200g/7oz drained weight)

1 slice of crustless bread

1 tablespoon red wine vinegar

Salt and pepper

SALSA

METHOD

1 Wash the tomatoes and chop them into halves.

2 Peel and chop the garlic and red onion.

3 Deseed the chilli and chop it into tiny pieces. (Do not touch your eyes when doing this and make sure you wash your hands thoroughly once you have finished chopping the chilli.)

4 Tip the tomatoes, garlic, red onion and chilli into a food processor.

5 Drain the peppers in a sieve, then chop them roughly. Tear up the bread into rough pieces.

6 Add the peppers and bread to the food processor along with the vinegar and a pinch of salt and pepper. Blend the ingredients by using the pulse button a few times to make a rough purée (it is not meant to be smooth).

7 Tip the salsa into a small bowl, cover it with cling film (plastic wrap) and chill until ready to serve.

 If you don't have a food processor, you can chop everything by hand into very small pieces and leave the bread out.

Makes 8 large sausage rolls

 Suitable for freezing

HOW TO:

SEALING & CRIMPING

SAUSAGE ROLLS

INGREDIENTS

1 egg

8 sausages/vegetarian sausages, or 350g (12oz) sausage meat

1 small onion

Salt and pepper

1 teaspoon thyme, fresh or dried (optional), plus extra to sprinkle

½ teaspoon caraway seeds (optional), plus extra to sprinkle

Flour, for rolling out pastry

2 x quantity shortcrust pastry (see page 178) or 1 x quantity rough puff pastry (see page 176), or 500g (1lb 2oz) shop-bought pastry

These sausage rolls are delicious hot or cold with mustard or tomato sauce.

METHOD

1   Preheat the oven to 200°C/400°F/Gas mark 7 and line a baking tray with baking parchment.

2   Crack the egg into a cup and beat it with a fork. If using sausages, remove and discard the skin of the sausages by cutting down the length of the sausage and peeling back the skin. Put the sausage meat in a bowl. Peel and finely chop the onion and add to the bowl with a pinch of salt and pepper. Add half of the beaten egg, as well as the thyme and caraway seeds if using.

3   Lightly sprinkle a work surface with flour and use a rolling pin to roll the pastry into a large rectangle, measuring approximately 40 x 30cm (16 x 12 inches). Cut the pastry in half lengthways to make two smaller rectangles, about 40 x 15cm (16 x 6 inches) each.

4   Mix together the sausage filling with your hands or a fork. Divide the mixture in half and form each half into a 40cm (16 inch) long sausage shape using your hands.

5   Place a long sausage onto a piece of the pastry. Wet the long side with a little bit of cold water and fold the pastry over the sausage meat to make one long sausage roll. 'Seal' the pastry properly by pressing the edges together or crimping the edge with your fingers or a fork. Cut into 4 even-sized sausage rolls (or cut them in half again to make 8 little sausage rolls).

6   Repeat step 5 with the remaining sausage and pastry so that you end up with 8 large sausage rolls (or 16 little sausage rolls) in total. Place them onto the baking tray.

7   Cut a slit in the top of the sausage rolls to allow steam to escape. Brush with the remainder of the egg and sprinkle with thyme and caraway seeds if using.

8   Bake the sausage rolls for 25–30 minutes (or 20–25 minutes if you have made 16 smaller rolls), or until the pastry is golden brown.

 Instead of thyme and caraway, you could sprinkle them with poppy or sesame seeds, or just leave them plain if you prefer.

Photographed with puff pastry, caraway seeds and thyme

Makes about 20 straws

 Suitable for freezing

Serve immediately, as they are delicious served warm.

INGREDIENTS

75g (2½oz) Cheddar or Parmesan cheese

Flour, for rolling out pastry

500g (1lb 2oz) rough puff pastry (see page 176) or shop-bought puff pastry

1 egg

2 sprigs fresh rosemary, roughly chopped (optional)

½ teaspoon salt (optional)

1 teaspoon paprika or mustard powder (optional)

CHEESE STRAWS

METHOD

1 Preheat the oven to 200°C/400°F/Gas mark 7. Line a baking tray with baking parchment. You may need to use two baking trays or cook them in two batches depending on the size of the baking tray.

2 Grate the cheese.

3 Lightly dust a work surface with a little bit of flour. Using a rolling pin, roll the rough puff pastry into a rectangle measuring approximately 30 x 20cm (12 x 8 inch).

4 Crack the egg into a cup and beat it with a fork, then brush the beaten egg all over the pastry.

5 Sprinkle the cheese over the pastry, spreading it out evenly and pressing it in lightly. Top with rosemary, salt and paprika or mustard powder, if using.

6 Cut the pastry widthways into 1.5cm (½ inch) wide strips and twist each one. Put them on the lined baking tray, pressing down each end so that it doesn't untwist.

7 Bake them in the oven for 15–17 minutes, or until they are golden and crisp.

 The cheese straws will keep for up to 3 days in an airtight container. To crisp them up, put them on a baking tray and put in a hot oven (200°C/400°F/Gas mark 7) for 2 minutes.

Photographed with rosemary

Serves 4

 Suitable for freezing

HOW TO:

SEALING & CRIMPING

CORNISH PASTIES

INGREDIENTS

1 tablespoon oil

200g (7oz) minced (ground) beef or Quorn

1 small onion

1 large potato (about 150g/5½oz)

1 carrot (about 75g/2½oz)

50g (1¾oz) frozen peas

Salt and pepper

Flour, for rolling out pastry

2 x quantity shortcrust pastry (see page 178) or 1 x 500g block shop-bought shortcrust pastry

A splash of milk, to glaze

These pasties are delicious served hot, with tomato sauce.

METHOD

1   Preheat the oven to 200°C/400°F/Gas mark 7.

2   Put the oil in a frying pan with the beef or Quorn and fry on a high heat, stirring with a wooden spoon until cooked through. This will take 5–10 minutes for beef (you shouldn't be able to see any pink) or 3 minutes for Quorn. Tip it into a mixing bowl.

3   Peel, then grate or finely chop the onion and add to the mixing bowl with the beef or Quorn. Peel, wash and grate the potato and carrot and add to the mixing bowl. Add the peas and season with salt and pepper. Mix it all together.

4   Lightly dust a work surface with flour. With a rolling pin, roll out the pastry until it is 2–3mm (¹⁄₁₆ inch) thick. Cut out 4 circles, each about 20cm (8 inch) in diameter, using a small plate or bowl to cut around.

5   Spoon one-quarter of the filling into the middle of each circle and brush the edge of the pasty with a little cold water.

6   Fold the circles in half to make semi-circular pasties and pinch the edges together to make a tight seal. Place them on a baking tray.

7   Using a sharp knife, pierce a hole in the top of each pasty to allow steam to escape during cooking.

8   Using a pastry brush, brush a little milk all over the tops to glaze.

9   Bake the pasties for 20–25 minutes, or until they are golden brown.

Photographed using beef mince

Makes 8 samosas

 Suitable for freezing

HOW TO:

FOLDING
SAMOSAS

SAMOSAS

INGREDIENTS

Oil, for greasing

1 medium potato
(about 100g/3½oz)

1 onion

200g (7oz) minced (ground)
lamb or Quorn

50g (1¾oz) frozen peas

1 teaspoon chilli powder

1 teaspoon ground cumin
(optional)

4 tablespoons oil

Salt and pepper

4 sheets filo (phyllo) pastry

Serve with raita or
mint sauce.

METHOD

1   Preheat the oven to 190°C/375°F/Gas mark 6 and lightly grease a baking tray with oil.

2   Peel and chop the potato into 1cm (½ inch) pieces.

3   Peel and finely chop the onion.

4   Put the minced lamb (or Quorn), potato, onion, peas, chilli powder and cumin, if using, into a frying pan with a tablespoon of the oil. Cook for about 12 minutes on a low–medium heat, stirring occasionally with a wooden spoon, until the mince is cooked through and there is no pink, and the potato is softening. If you're using Quorn, cook until the potato is softening. Leave the filling to cool. Add a pinch of salt and pepper.

5   Cut the filo pastry sheets in half lengthways, creating 8 long rectangles. Place one pastry rectangle in front of you with a short edge towards you and cover the remainder of the pastry with a clean, damp cloth (either a J cloth or a tea towel) when not using.

6   Brush the edge of the pastry with oil, about 1cm (½ inch) all the way around the edge. Put a tablespoonful of filling into the bottom corner of the pastry and fold the edges over to make a triangle. Continue to fold it up in the triangle shape until you have used up the rectangle of filo and the parcel is sealed on all sides.

7   Place on the baking tray with the seal of the samosa facing down, then repeat to fold the remaining samosas.

8   Bake in the oven for 5–8 minutes, or until golden brown.

 Traditionally, these are deep fried in oil, but it is healthier to bake them and you still end up with a crispy casing.

Photographed with lamb mince and mint sauce

NAAN BREAD

HOW TO:

KNEADING
DOUGH

METHOD

1   For the dough, put the flour, sugar, salt and baking powder into a bowl.

2   In a measuring jug, mix together the milk and the oil.

3   Make a well in the centre of the flour mixture and pour in the liquid mixture. Slowly mix together the ingredients until a soft dough forms. Knead it well for 5–10 minutes.

4   Split the dough into 6 balls.

5   On a floured surface, roll the dough balls out thinly, ideally in a teardrop shape.

6   Heat the grill (broiler) to medium and place the naans under the grill for 1–2 minutes, or until lightly browned. Alternatively, fry them one at a time in a frying pan on a medium heat, with a teaspoon of oil per naan. Fry them for 2–3 minutes on each side, until golden brown.

7   Brush with butter or oil, and add the topping of your choice.

INGREDIENTS

250g (9oz) plain (all-purpose) flour, plus extra for dusting

2 teaspoons sugar

½ teaspoon salt

½ teaspoon baking powder

120ml (4fl oz) milk

2 tablespoons vegetable oil (plus extra if frying)

For the topping

25g (1oz) butter, or 2 tablespoons oil

1 tablespoon chopped garlic or 1 tablespoon chopped coriander (cilantro) or 1 tablespoon desiccated (dried shredded) coconut (all optional)

Serve hot as an accompaniment to a curry (see page 64), or with mango chutney.

Photographed with mango chutney

Makes 8 rolls

 Suitable for freezing

HOW TO:

KNEADING
DOUGH

BREAD ROLLS

METHOD

1 Preheat the oven to 200°C/400°F/Gas mark 7. Get a baking tray and lightly sprinkle it with flour (this will stop the rolls sticking to the tray).

2 Put the flour, yeast, oil and salt into a mixing bowl and mix together with a butter knife.

3 Add the warm water and mix the dough using the knife. Then use one hand and bring the dough together into a ball.

4 Sprinkle some flour lightly onto a work surface and put your ball of dough onto it. Knead the dough for 5 minutes.

5 Cut the dough into 8 equal pieces and shape them into balls. Place them on the baking tray. Brush the rolls with oil using a pastry brush, and sprinkle with poppy or sesame seeds, if desired. Leave them in a warm place, such as on top of the oven, until they have doubled in size – ideally about half an hour.

6 Once they have doubled in size, bake them in the oven for 10–15 minutes, until they turn golden brown.

 You may need to add a little more warm water if using wholemeal flour, as it absorbs more water than white flour. At the end of step 4, you can add additional ingredients such as chopped olives, raisins and hazelnuts, chopped sundried tomatoes or finely chopped onion that has been fried in a little oil until golden brown. You can also make other shapes from your bread rolls, as long as they are all roughly the same size.

INGREDIENTS

250g (9oz) strong bread flour (white or wholemeal), plus extra for dusting

1 teaspoons dry yeast or ½ packet quick acting dried yeast

2 tablespoon oil, plus extra for brushing

½ teaspoon salt

150ml (5¼fl oz) warm water (100ml/3½fl oz cold mixed with 50ml/1¾fl oz boiling)

Poppy or sesame seeds (optional)

These rolls are best served warm.

Photographed with poppy seeds, fried onions and plain

Makes 16–24 rolls

 Suitable for freezing

HOW TO:

SHAPING
SPRING
ROLLS

SPRING ROLLS

INGREDIENTS

4 tablespoons vegetable oil, plus extra for greasing

125g (4½oz) minced (ground) pork, chicken or Quorn

2 teaspoons soy sauce

200g (7oz) vegetables, such as spring onions (scallions), beansprouts, mushrooms, Chinese cabbage or carrots

4-6 sheets filo (phyllo) pastry

Serve with sweet chilli sauce or hoisin sauce.

METHOD

1   Preheat the oven to 190°C/375°F/Gas mark 6. Grease a baking tray with oil.

2   Put the minced meat or Quorn into a small bowl and mix in the soy sauce with a spoon.

3   Wash and prepare the vegetables. Finely chop the spring onions. Thinly slice the mushrooms and cabbage. Peel and cut the carrots into matchstick-sized pieces.

4   Put a tablespoon of the oil into a frying pan and add the meat or Quorn mixture. Fry on a high heat for 3–5 minutes, stirring continuously and breaking up the mince. If using Quorn, just fry for 2 minutes.

5   Add the vegetables and cook for a further 3 minutes, making sure the meat is cooked through, then take the pan off the heat and allow the mixture to cool slightly.

6   Cut the filo pastry sheets in half lengthways, creating long rectangles. Place one pastry rectangle in front of you with a short edge towards you and cover the remainder of the pastry with a clean, damp cloth (either a J cloth or a tea towel) when not using.

7   Spoon 1 heaped tablespoon of filling onto the pastry, arranging it in a small sausage shape along the bottom edge.

8   Roll the pastry up until three-quarters of the way up. Brush the edge with oil and fold in the sides. Then continue to roll up. Make sure all the filling is tucked in tightly!

9   Place on the baking tray with the seal of the spring roll facing down, then repeat to fold the remaining spring rolls.

10 Bake in the oven for approximately 5–8 minutes until golden brown in colour.

 You can add some finely chopped fresh ginger and/ or 1 tablespoon of chopped coriander (cilantro) to the mixture at the end of step 5, if you like.

Photographed with pork mince and sweet chilli sauce

Serve with sweet chilli sauce or Vietnamese style dipping sauce.

SUMMER ROLLS
VIETNAMESE STYLE

INGREDIENTS

100g (3½oz) rice vermicelli noodles

150g (5½oz) prepared vegetables (choose 3 of the following: spring onions (scallions), carrots, cucumber, iceberg lettuce, red cabbage – about 50g/1¾oz of each)

50g (1¾oz) beansprouts

Small bunch of coriander (cilantro)

Small bunch of Thai basil

Small bunch of mint

18 large cooked prawns (shrimp) or 36 small cooked prawns (optional)

12 rice paper wrappers (approx. 20cm/8 inch wide)

METHOD

1   Put the noodles in a bowl, cover with boiling water and leave for 15 minutes (or as per the instructions on the packet).

2   While the noodles are soaking, wash and cut your chosen vegetables into very thin strips, about 7cm (2¾ inch) long.

3   Wash the beansprouts in a colander or sieve.

4   Wash and dry the coriander, Thai basil and mint. Take the Thai basil and mint leaves off their stalks.

5   If you are using large prawns, cut them in half lengthways.

6   Drain the rice noodles in a colander or sieve.

7   Fill a large mixing bowl with warm water. Dip a rice paper wrapper into the water and move it around until it is soft all over (about 10 seconds), then carefully lift it onto a chopping board or large plate and spread it out flat.

8   Add a few herbs just in from the edge of the wrapper, followed by some noodles, strips of vegetables and a few beansprouts, then add 3 large prawn halves or 3 small prawns, if using.

9   Pick up the edge of the rice paper closest to you and place over the filling, holding the filling tight as you roll. When you have rolled the wrapper two-thirds of the way up, fold in the left and right sides to enclose the filling, then continue to roll up to the end. The wrapper will stick to itself to seal the filling in. Repeat to fill all the wrappers.

10 Store in the fridge and eat within 24 hours.

   Don't overfill the rolls as they will be difficult to roll up and may tear.

Photographed with prawns and Vietnamese style dipping sauce

4 Serves 4

 Saucepan with lid

 Sushi rolling mat

Serve with pickled ginger, soy sauce, sesame seeds and wasabi.

INGREDIENTS

250g (9oz) sushi rice

330ml (11¼fl oz) cold water

2 tablespoons rice wine vinegar

Fillings – choose 2 or 3 of the following: ½ cucumber, 1 raw carrot, 1 avocado, 100g/3½oz smoked salmon, 100g/3½oz fresh sushi-grade salmon or tuna, 100g/3½oz prawns (shrimp)

4 sheets of nori (seaweed)

To serve (all optional)

Pickled ginger

Soy sauce

Sesame seeds

Wasabi

SUSHI
MAKI ROLLS

METHOD

1   Put the rice in a large saucepan and pour in the cold water. Turn on the heat to high and bring to the boil. Once boiling, lower the heat and put the lid on. Simmer for 10 minutes. Turn off the heat and leave to steam with the lid on for a further 10 minutes. (Alternatively, follow the instructions on the packet of sushi rice.)

2   Empty the cooked rice into a bowl, add the rice wine vinegar and mix in. Cover the bowl with cling film and chill in the fridge until the rice is cold.

3   To prepare your fillings, cut everything into thin strips. Cut the cucumber and carrot into matchsticks, and any other ingredients, such as avocado, salmon, tuna or prawns, should be cut into 1cm (½ inch) thick strips.

4   Place a sheet of nori, shiny side down, onto the rolling mat.

5   With slightly wet hands, pick up one-quarter of the rice and arrange it over the nori sheet in a layer about 3mm (⅛ inch) thick. Cover the entire sheet, but leave a 4cm (1½ inch) strip bare at the top, patting the rice down to ensure it is an even layer, and making sure the rice goes right to the three edges.

6   Arrange the fillings in a horizontal line across the rice, about a third of the way up.

7   Roll the sushi up, keeping the roll as tight as possible, towards the bare strip of nori at the top. As you get to the end, wet the strip of nori with a little water and continue rolling to seal the end. Repeat with the remaining nori sheets and ingredients. If you have time, place the sushi rolls in the fridge to chill before cutting them.

8   Carefully lift the rolls onto a chopping board and, with a slightly wet knife, cut the rolls into even-sized pieces, about 2cm (¾ inch) wide. You need a very sharp knife for this in order for it to be neat.

 This takes longer than 1 hour as you have to let the rice cool during the recipe. Don't lift the lid off the rice while it's cooking! Cover the rolling mat in cling film (plastic wrap) so it doesn't get covered in rice. If you haven't got a rolling mat then you can use a piece of foil covered in cling film instead, but you may have to use a new one for each roll you make as it can crumple easily.

Photographed with sushi-grade salmon, avocado and cucumber, accompanied by pickled ginger, soy sauce and wasabi

4 Serves 4

Delicious on its own or served with grilled (broiled) or barbecued meats, fish or halloumi.

INGREDIENTS

150g (5½oz) couscous

250ml (9fl oz) boiling water

2 medium tomatoes

1 red or yellow (bell) pepper

4 spring onions (scallions)

3 tablespoons fresh herbs (any combination of parsley, mint and/or coriander/cilantro)

3 tablespoons olive or sunflower oil

2 tablespoons lemon juice

Salt and pepper

COUSCOUS SALAD

METHOD

1 Put the couscous in a mixing bowl and pour the boiling water over it. Cover the bowl with cling film (plastic wrap) before leaving it to stand for 5 minutes. The couscous is ready once all the water has been absorbed.

2 While waiting for the couscous to absorb the water, wash and dice the tomatoes.

3 Use a fork to 'fluff up' the couscous.

4 Add the chopped tomatoes to the bowl.

5 Wash, deseed and chop the peppers into small pieces and add them to the bowl.

6 Chop the spring onions into small pieces, then chop the fresh herbs and add them both to the bowl.

7 Add the oil and lemon juice to the couscous. Finish by adding a pinch of salt and pepper to taste.

8 Serve immediately or refrigerate until required.

 This is a cold dish, however if you'd prefer to serve it warm, roast the tomatoes, peppers and onions for 20–30 minutes in the oven at 180°C/350°F/Gas mark 6, then mix them in.

Serves 4

 Suitable for freezing

 Saucepan with lid

Serve hot on its own, or as a side dish with a roast dinner.

VEGETABLES IN A CHEESE SAUCE

INGREDIENTS

1 cauliflower or 500g (1lb 2oz) broccoli or 500g (1lb 2oz) leeks

1 quantity of White Sauce with cheese (see page 172)

50g (1¾oz) breadcrumbs (optional)

50g (1¾oz) Cheddar or Parmesan cheese (optional)

METHOD

1   Preheat the oven to 180°C/350°F/Gas mark 6.

2   Wash your chosen vegetable and chop: take the outer leaves off the cauliflower and cut it up into small florets; or cut the broccoli up into small florets; or cut the ends off the leeks and chop them into 2cm (¾ inch) slices.

3   Put the vegetables into a saucepan (that has a lid). Pour boiling water over the top of the vegetables until it is just covering them, then bring the water to the boil on a high heat. Turn down to low and simmer with the lid on for 7 minutes.

4   Drain the vegetables carefully over the sink, using a sieve or colander.

5   Tip the vegetables into an ovenproof dish or a small roasting tin.

6   Make the white sauce following the recipe on page 172 and pour it over the vegetables.

7   Sprinkle with the breadcrumbs, if using – this gives the dish a nice, crunchy topping.

8   Grate the cheese, if using, and sprinkle it over the top. Put the dish in the oven and bake for 25 minutes until it starts to go golden brown.

 You can make this into macaroni cheese by swapping the vegetables for 350g (12oz) dried macaroni pasta and following the instructions from step 3, cooking the macaroni according to the instructions on the packet.

Photographed with cauliflower, breadcrumbs and Parmesan

MAIN
MEALS

6 Serves 6

 Suitable for freezing

You can add any extras you like to your burgers, such as sliced avocado or cooked bacon.

INGREDIENTS

1 small onion

1 egg

500g (1lb 2oz) minced (ground) beef, lamb or Quorn

1 teaspoon mixed dried herbs (or 1 tablespoon chopped fresh parsley)

Salt and pepper

A little oil, if frying

6 burger buns

Toppings (optional)

6 slices cheese

6 slices tomato

6 lettuce leaves

6 gherkins, sliced thinly

50g (1¾oz) red cabbage, sliced thinly

Ketchup/burger sauce

BURGERS

METHOD

1 Peel and finely chop the onion.

2 Beat the egg with a fork in a cup.

3 Put the onion, egg, meat or Quorn and herbs into a mixing bowl and season with salt and pepper. Mix it together with a fork or with your hands.

4 Divide the mixture into 6 equal portions. Shape them into burger patties by making a ball first and then flattening them, making sure that they are all the same size and the same thickness. (Or you can use a 10cm/4 inch round cookie cutter, pushing the ball of mixture into the cutter to shape it.)

5 Cook the burgers – either in a frying pan with a little oil over a medium heat, under the grill (broiler), or on a barbecue – for about 6 minutes on each side. Check that the burgers are cooked all the way through, that there is no pink in the middle and that they are piping hot.

6 Place each burger in a bun and top it with optional fillings.

 You could put the toppings into separate bowls for people to build their own! You can individually wrap raw burgers and put in the freezer. Defrost thoroughly before cooking.

Photographed with beef mince, gherkins, red cabbage, tomato, cheese, lettuce and burger sauce

Serves 4

 Suitable for freezing

 Saucepan with lid

Best served with rice, mango chutney and naan bread (see page 46).

INGREDIENTS

1 onion

1 garlic clove

2 tablespoons olive oil

4 chicken breasts or 500g/1lb 2oz Quorn chunks

1 x 400ml (14oz) can of coconut milk

2 teaspoons curry powder

2 tablespoons tomato purée (tomato paste)

Salt and pepper

2 tablespoons chopped fresh coriander (cilantro) (optional)

CURRY
INDIAN STYLE

METHOD

1 Peel the onion and chop into small pieces. Peel and finely chop (or crush) the garlic.

2 In a large saucepan, fry the onion and garlic for about 2 minutes in the olive oil on a medium heat until they are soft, stirring constantly with a wooden spoon.

3 Chop the chicken breasts into small pieces. Add the chicken to the onions and garlic and fry, stirring frequently, continuing on a medium heat, until it is cooked all the way through (this will take about 8 minutes, depending on the size of the pieces). Alternatively, add the Quorn and fry for 4 minutes.

4 Add the coconut milk and curry powder and stir through. Simmer the curry over a low heat for 15 minutes with the lid on.

5 Remove the lid and stir in the tomato purée. Continue cooking with the lid off for about 3 minutes, stirring occasionally, until the sauce thickens slightly.

6 Add salt and pepper to taste.

7 If using, wash and chop the coriander and scatter over the curry to serve.

Photographed with naan bread

Serves 4

 Suitable for freezing

Serve with summer noodle salad (see page 102) and a wedge of lime.

CHICKEN

THAI STYLE

INGREDIENTS

4 garlic cloves

4cm (1½ inch) piece of fresh root ginger

100ml (3½fl oz) soy sauce

2 tablespoons honey

1 tablespoon sesame oil

1 teaspoon chilli flakes

8 chicken thighs

1 tablespoon sesame seeds

METHOD

1 Preheat the oven to 180°C/350°F/Gas mark 6.

2 Peel and finely chop the garlic and ginger.

3 Mix all of the ingredients, except the chicken thighs and sesame seeds, together in a large mixing bowl, then add the chicken thighs. Cover the bowl with cling film (plastic wrap) and leave it to marinate for at least 30 minutes in the fridge.

4 Remove the cling film and lay the chicken thighs out on a baking tray. Pour the remaining marinade over the top and place the tray in the oven.

5 Roast the chicken for 45 minutes, basting with the juices (spoon the juices over the top of the chicken) halfway through cooking.

6 Take the chicken out of the oven and sprinkle the sesame seeds over.

 This dish can also be cooked on a barbecue instead of roasting – just make sure the chicken is cooked all the way through. If you freeze this chicken dish, make sure to defrost thoroughly before reheating.

Photographed with summer noodle salad and a wedge of lime

Serves 4

 Suitable for freezing

 Saucepan with lid

CHILLI CON CARNE

Great served with rice, sour cream and fresh coriander (cilantro).

INGREDIENTS

1 onion

2 garlic cloves

1 tablespoon olive oil

500g (1lb 2oz) minced beef or Quorn

2 red (bell) peppers

1 red chilli

1 x 400g (14oz) can of chopped tomatoes

1 tablespoon tomato purée (tomato paste) (optional)

1 x 400g (14oz) can of kidney beans, rinsed, or 1 can baked beans (optional)

1 teaspoon ground cumin

1 teaspoon sugar

Salt and pepper

METHOD

1   Peel and chop the onion and garlic.

2   Put the oil into a large saucepan and fry the onion and garlic until golden brown and soft – about 3 minutes on a medium heat. Use a wooden spoon to stir it occasionally.

3   Add the minced beef and cook thoroughly, stirring, for about 6 minutes, until you can't see any pink. If using Quorn, cook it for 4 minutes.

4   Deseed the red peppers and chop them into roughly 1cm (½ inch) pieces, then add them to the pan. Deseed the chilli and chop it as finely as you can. Add the chilli to the pan, along with the tomatoes and tomato purée (if using). Put the lid on the pan, turn the heat down to low and cook for 20 minutes.

5   Add the remaining ingredients with a pinch of salt and pepper, and stir them in. Leave the lid off and cook for a further 5 minutes to thicken up the sauce.

 Remember to wash your hands thoroughly after chopping the chilli. Freeze portions in individual pots and serve on a jacket potato for a quick meal.

Photographed with kidney beans

6 Serves 6

 Suitable for freezing

 Saucepan with lid

SHEPHERD'S PIE

INGREDIENTS

For the base

1 tablespoon oil

2 onions

1 stick celery (optional)

2 carrots (optional)

500g (1lb 2oz) minced (ground) lamb or Quorn

1 x 400g (14oz) can of chopped tomatoes

1 stock cube (lamb, beef or vegetable)

3 tablespoons tomato purée (tomato paste)

2 teaspoons dried mixed herbs

Salt and pepper

2 teaspoons mint jelly (optional)

150g (5½oz) frozen peas (optional)

1 small can sweetcorn (optional)

For the topping

1 x quantity mashed potato (see page 174)

25g (1oz) Cheddar cheese (optional)

METHOD

1 Make the mashed potato for the topping, following the recipe on page 174. While the potatoes are boiling, start on the pie base.

2 Preheat the oven to 180°C/350°F/Gas mark 6.

3 Put the oil in a saucepan (that has a lid). Peel and chop the onions and put into the saucepan with the oil.

4 Prepare the celery and carrot, if using: wash the celery, then chop into small pieces; wash, peel and grate the carrot.

5 Heat the oil and onions over a medium heat and stir with a wooden spoon for 5 minutes, or until soft and golden.

6 Add the minced lamb or Quorn to the saucepan, stirring to break up any lumps. Cook for about 6 minutes, or until any red colour has gone from the meat (or if using Quorn, cook according to the instructions on the packet).

7 Add the carrot and celery, if using, and stir in.

8 Add the canned tomatoes, stock cube, tomato purée and mixed herbs. Add a pinch of salt and pepper.

9 Allow to simmer on a low heat for 10 minutes with the lid on until the sauce thickens slightly. Stir occasionally so that the mixture doesn't stick to the bottom of the pan.

10 Add the mint jelly, peas and sweetcorn to the sauce, if using, and stir in for 2 minutes.

11 Pour the meat sauce into an ovenproof dish or small roasting tin. Carefully spoon the mashed potato over the top of the sauce and use a fork to level it out and make a lined pattern on the top. Grate the Cheddar cheese, if using, and sprinkle over the top of the mashed potato. Cook in the oven for 20 minutes until the potato is golden brown.

 This takes longer than 1 hour as you have to make the mashed potato recipe first. To make a cottage pie instead, use minced (ground) beef and leave out the mint jelly.

Photographed with lamb mince, peas and sweetcorn

Serves 6

 Suitable for freezing

 Saucepan with lid

Serve with grated Parmesan or Cheddar cheese.

INGREDIENTS

1 onion

2 garlic cloves

3 tablespoons olive oil

250g (9oz) minced (ground) beef (or Quorn)

1 x 400g (14oz) can of chopped tomatoes

2 tablespoons tomato purée (tomato paste)

1 stock cube (beef or vegetable)

1 teaspoon mixed herbs or dried oregano

400g (14oz) dried spaghetti or 500g (1lb 2oz) fresh spaghetti

Salt and pepper

SPAGHETTI BOLOGNESE

METHOD

1 Peel and chop the onion and garlic.

2 In a large saucepan (that has a lid), fry the onion and garlic in the oil on a medium heat for about 5 minutes, until soft.

3 Add the minced beef and cook, stirring and breaking it up with a wooden spoon, for about 8 minutes until it's brown all the way through and there is no pink meat. If you are using Quorn, add it to the pan and stir for 5 minutes over a medium heat.

4 Add the chopped tomatoes, tomato purée, stock cube and herbs and stir in.

5 Bring the sauce to the boil, then turn it down to a simmer. Put a lid on the saucepan and leave it for 20 minutes, stirring occasionally so that it doesn't stick to the bottom of the saucepan.

6 While your Bolognese sauce is simmering, bring a large saucepan of water to the boil. Put the spaghetti in the saucepan and bring the water back to the boil. Turn the heat down and simmer for about 10 minutes if dried, or about 4 minutes if fresh (check packaging for cooking instructions). Drain the pasta in a colander or sieve over the sink.

7 Season the meat sauce with salt and pepper.

8 Portion the spaghetti into bowls and top with the Bolognese sauce.

 You can add grated carrot, thinly sliced celery or grated courgette (zucchini) at step 4 to make your Bolognese healthier.

Serves 4

 Suitable for freezing

These can be eaten hot or cold, either as a meal on their own or as a side dish.

INGREDIENTS

70g (2½oz) couscous

100ml (3½fl oz) boiling water

1 small onion or 1 small leek

1 tablespoon oil

2 tablespoons fresh mint or basil

40g (2½oz) sultanas (optional)

40g (2½oz) pine nuts (optional)

1 tablespoon balsamic vinegar

2 (bell) peppers (any colour)

50g (1¾oz) Cheddar/ mozzarella/feta

STUFFED PEPPERS

METHOD

1   Preheat the oven to 190°C/375°F/Gas mark 6.

2   Put the couscous in a bowl and add the boiling water. Cover it in cling film (plastic wrap) and leave it for at least 5 minutes.

3   While the couscous is absorbing the water, peel the onion and chop it into small pieces, or wash and chop the leek finely.

4   Put the oil in a small saucepan or frying pan and cook the onion/ leek on a medium heat until it is soft and starting to go golden, stirring with a wooden spoon (approximately 3 minutes).

5   Take the cling film off the couscous and fluff it up with a fork.

6   Chop the mint or basil and add it to the 'fluffed up' couscous with the onion/leek, sultanas and pine nuts, if using, and balsamic vinegar, and mix it all together.

7   Slice the peppers through the middle, keeping half the stalk on each side. Remove the seeds and put the peppers into an ovenproof dish or small roasting tin.

8   Spoon the couscous mixture into the peppers. Grate or chop the cheese into small pieces and sprinkle on the top of each pepper.

9   Cook them in the oven for approximately 20 minutes until the skin of the peppers 'blisters' and browns slightly.

Photographed with sultanas, pine nuts and feta

FAJITAS

HOW TO:

HALVE AND STONE AN AVOCADO

INGREDIENTS

2 onions

4 tablespoons olive oil

4 chicken breasts (or 500g/1lb 2oz Quorn chunks)

2 red (bell) peppers (or 1 red and 1 yellow)

1 x 28g (1oz) pack of fajita spice mix or 1 tablespoon Cajun spice mix

8 tortilla wraps

For the toppings

½ bunch coriander (cilantro)

100g (3½oz) Cheddar or Monterey Jack cheese (optional)

2 limes

½ iceberg lettuce

1 avocado (optional)

250ml (9oz) sour cream

METHOD

1   Prepare the toppings first and put them each in a separate bowl: chop the coriander; grate the cheese; cut each lime into 4 wedges; cut the lettuce into thin strips; stone and chop the avocado into small pieces.

2   Peel and slice the onions into thin strips. Heat the oil in a large frying pan and cook the onions on a medium heat until they are soft and golden.

3   Cut the chicken breasts into small pieces and add to the frying pan. (If using Quorn, add now and cook for 2 minutes, then skip to step 4.) Cook the chicken breasts for about 10 minutes on a medium heat, stirring often with a wooden spoon, until there is no pink showing in the middle of the meat. Wash up thoroughly anything that has come into contact with the raw chicken, such as the chopping board and the knife.

4   Prepare the peppers by deseeding them and removing the stalks, then cut them into thin slices and add to the frying pan. Fry for a further 5 minutes.

5   Sprinkle the fajita or Cajun spice over the top and stir in, and continue to fry on a medium heat for 1 minute.

6   Take off the heat and serve with the prepared toppings and tortilla wraps.

 Get everyone to assemble their own wraps. Start with a tortilla on a plate and spread a tablespoon of sour cream over it. Add the lettuce and hot chicken mixture, then top with cheese, avocado and coriander. Roll up the wrap, folding in the bottom as well as the sides so the filling doesn't fall out when you eat it. For a low-carb option, serve the fajitas in lettuce leaves instead of wraps.

This can also be served with half a portion of tomato salsa (see page 36).

FISH & CHIPS

Serve with peas
and tartare sauce.

INGREDIENTS

2 tablespoons oil

2 medium-sized white
    potatoes or sweet potatoes

1 teaspoon chilli flakes
    (optional)

1 egg

50g (1¾oz) fresh
    breadcrumbs

Salt and pepper

2 boneless fish fillets (such
    as cod, hake, plaice,
    salmon)

2 lemon wedges or slices

METHOD

1   Preheat the oven to 180°C/350°F/Gas mark 6. Grease a baking tray
    with half of the oil.

2   Cut the potatoes into chips (batons), about 1cm (½ inch) thick.

3   Place your chips onto the baking tray and brush the remaining oil over
    them. Sprinkle with chilli flakes (if using). Put the chips in the oven for
    20 minutes.

4   While the chips are cooking, crack the egg into a small bowl and beat
    it with a fork.

5   Put the breadcrumbs on a plate, add a pinch of salt and pepper and
    mix together.

6   Dip a fish fillet into the egg, making sure that you coat it fully. Then
    put it in the breadcrumbs and roll it over in order to coat the whole
    fillet. Repeat with the other fillet.

7   Take the chips out of the oven and turn them over using a fish slice.
    Place the fish fillets onto the same baking tray and put it back into the
    oven to continue to cook for a further 20 minutes, or until the fish is
    cooked.

8   Serve immediately with a wedge or slice of lemon.

❋   The cooking time will vary depending on the thickness
    of the fish. Check the thickest part is cooked – it should
    be opaque rather than translucent and flake easily.
    This technique of breadcrumbing can be used with
    chicken breast (which needs about 30 minutes to cook),
    courgette (zucchini) slices or halloumi, too.

Photographed with sweet potato fries

Serves 4
(makes 8 kebabs)

 8 kebab skewers
(wooden or metal)

Serve in hot pitta pockets or with a couscous salad (see page 56).

INGREDIENTS

1 red (bell) pepper

1 yellow (bell) pepper

1 courgette (zucchini)

1 small red onion

200g (7oz) halloumi cheese (optional)

For the marinade

1 garlic clove

2 tablespoons soy sauce

1 teaspoon honey

1 tablespoon oil

Salt and pepper

KEBABS

METHOD

1 Cut the red pepper into 8 even pieces, and the yellow pepper into 8 even pieces, so that you have 16 pieces of pepper in total, discarding the seeds and stalks.

2 Slice the ends off the courgette, then cut it into 16 thin slices.

3 Peel and cut the red onion into 8 wedges.

4 Cut the halloumi into 8 cubes, if using.

5 Peel and finely chop the garlic, or crush it using a garlic crusher.

6 Combine all the marinade ingredients in a bowl and mix together.

7 Thread the vegetables and halloumi, if using, onto 8 skewers, dividing everything equally between the skewers. Place on a baking tray or plate and pour the marinade over the kebabs.

8 Grill or barbecue the kebabs for about 10 minutes, turning occasionally, until the vegetables are cooked. Alternatively, you can cook these on a baking tray in an oven set to 180°C/350°F/Gas mark 6 for 20–25 minutes.

 These can be prepared in advance, covered in cling film (plastic wrap) and left in the fridge for up to 6 hours before cooking. You can swap the halloumi for 2 chicken breasts or 200g (7oz) beef or lamb, diced into cubes. Make sure the meat is cooked all the way through (this will take about 20 minutes on a barbecue or grill and 30 minutes in the oven).

Photographed with halloumi

Serve immediately while piping hot.

NOODLE STIR FRY

METHOD

1   Peel and chop the carrot into thin sticks. Cut the broccoli into florets (small pieces). Peel and finely chop the ginger and garlic. Deseed the peppers and slice them into thin strips. Leave the mangetout and beansprouts whole.

2   Heat the oil in a wok or large frying pan on a medium heat.

3   Add the carrot and broccoli to the pan and stir with a wooden spoon for 2 minutes.

4   Add the ginger and garlic to the pan and stir for a further 1 minute.

5   Add the peppers and mangetout and stir for about 4 minutes until they start to soften.

6   Add the beansprouts, noodles, soy sauce and honey, and stir for a final 2 minutes until everything is piping hot.

 You can vary the ingredients depending on what you like. You can also add prawns (shrimp), chicken, beef strips or tofu. If adding, cook them first and put into a bowl while you cook the vegetables, then return to the pan in step 6 to heat through.

INGREDIENTS

1 carrot

100g (3½oz) broccoli

2cm (¾ inch) piece of fresh root ginger

1 garlic clove

1 red (bell) pepper

1 yellow (bell) pepper

50g (1¾oz) mangetout (snow peas)

300g (10½oz) beansprouts

1 tablespoon olive oil

400g (14oz) cooked egg noodles or flat rice noodles

2 tablespoons soy sauce

2 tablespoons honey

Serve each portion with 1 chicken breast (or 2 thighs) and a selection of vegetables, with the juices poured over the top.

ONE PAN ROAST DINNER

METHOD

1   Preheat the oven to 180°C/350°F/Gas mark 6. Put the oil into a baking tray.

2   Peel and chop the onion into 4 wedges and put on the baking tray. Add the chicken breasts or thighs. Remove the thyme leaves from the sprig and sprinkle over the chicken. Cut the new potatoes in half and add to the baking tray. Toss all the ingredients in the baking tray with the oil so everything is coated. Put in the oven for 10 minutes.

3   While the chicken is starting to cook, peel and trim off the ends of the carrots and parsnips, then cut them into thin strips. Carefully take the baking tray out of the oven using oven gloves and add the carrots and parsnips to it, tossing in the oil. Put the baking tray back in the oven for a further 35 minutes.

4   Remove the tray from the oven again, and add the tenderstem broccoli or frozen peas and the water to the baking tray and cook for a further 8 minutes.

5   Take the dish out of the oven and spoon over some of the juices from the baking tray.

 You can use most types of meat, as long as it is in small cuts so that it cooks all the way through. If using lamb chops, add a sprig of rosemary instead of thyme, or for pork chops add a sprig of sage instead of thyme.

INGREDIENTS

2 tablespoons olive oil

1 red or white onion

4 skin-on chicken breasts or 8 chicken thighs

2 sprigs thyme (optional)

8 new potatoes

4 carrots

4 parsnips

8 tenderstem broccoli stems or 200g (7oz) frozen peas

4 tablespoons water

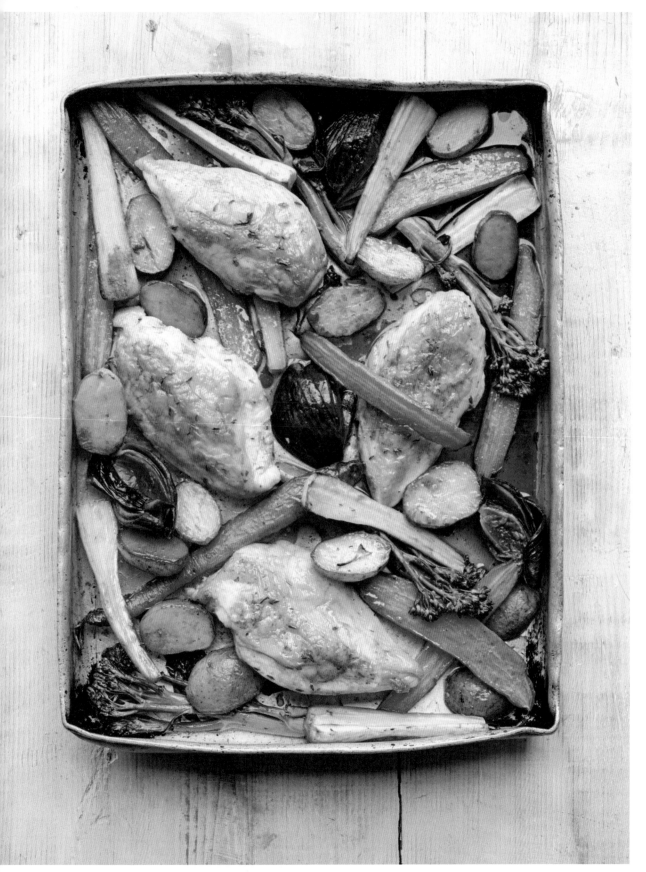

Photographed with chicken breasts, thyme and tenderstem broccoli

4 Serves 4
(makes 8 fish cakes)

 Suitable for freezing

Serve with green beans or a salad.

INGREDIENTS

1 tablespoon oil

1 x quantity of mashed
potato (see page 174)

2 tablespoons chopped
parsley, coriander (cilantro)
or dill

2 spring onions (scallions)

2 x 145g (5oz) cans of tuna
or salmon, drained,
or 300g (10½oz) white
crab meat

Salt and pepper

150g (5½oz) breadcrumbs

1 egg

FISH CAKES

METHOD

1 Preheat the oven to 200°C/400°F/Gas mark 7. Grease a baking tray with oil.

2 Make the mashed potato, following the recipe on page 174.

3 Finely chop the herbs. Wash and finely chop the spring onions.

4 Add the tuna or salmon, chopped herbs, spring onions and a pinch of salt and pepper to the mashed potato and mix it together.

5 Divide the mixture into 8 equal portions. Shape each one into a round ball, then flatten it slightly to make a round patty.

6 Put the breadcrumbs on a plate.

7 Crack the egg into a small bowl and beat it with a fork.

8 Coat each fishcake by dipping it first in the egg, then in the breadcrumbs, coating each one all over.

9 Place the fish cakes on the greased baking tray and bake them in the oven for 20 minutes, or until crisp and golden brown.

 If you want to spice it up, add a finely chopped chilli to the fish mixture, or a pinch of paprika or cayenne pepper. As an alternative to oven baking, these fish cakes can be shallow fried in a little oil for 2–3 minutes on each side.

Photographed with salmon

PAELLA

Serve with 2 tablespoons of chopped fresh parsley and 4 lemon wedges.

INGREDIENTS

2 small onions

1 red (bell) pepper

1 garlic clove

2 tablespoons olive oil

120g (4¼oz) chorizo (optional)

Pinch of saffron

1 teaspoon paprika

300g (10½oz) paella rice

1 stock cube dissolved in 650ml (22½fl oz) boiling water

200g (7oz) frozen peas

160g (5¾oz) canned sweetcorn

METHOD

1   Peel and finely chop the onions. Wash, deseed and dice the pepper and peel and crush or finely chop the garlic.

2   Heat the oil in a large frying pan or paella pan on a medium heat. Add the onions and cook until they are soft and lightly golden, about 5 minutes.

3   Add the red pepper and garlic and stir for 1 minute.

4   Chop the chorizo, if using, and add to the frying pan. Fry for 1–2 minutes until it releases its oils.

5   Stir in the saffron and paprika, then add the rice and stir so that the rice is coated in the oils and spices. Pour in the stock, turn the heat down to low, and simmer for about 20 minutes, stirring occasionally. If it becomes too dry, add 100ml (3½fl oz) more water. You need to be patient at this stage!

6   Add the peas. Drain the sweetcorn in a sieve and add to the pan, then simmer for a further 5 minutes on a low heat until the rice is cooked. Try a mouthful and check that the rice is soft. If it isn't, cook for a further 5 minutes.

 You can also add cooked chicken, prawns (shrimp), squid, mussels or scallops in step 6 – just make sure that the extra ingredients are piping hot before serving.

Photographed with prawns, mussels and no peas

Serves 4
(makes 2 large pizzas)

 Suitable for freezing

Serve with a green
side salad.

INGREDIENTS

300g (10½oz) self-raising
flour, plus extra for dusting

1 teaspoon baking powder

½ teaspoon salt

300g (10½oz) natural yoghurt

1 tablespoon oil, for greasing

4 tablespoons tomato purée
(tomato paste)

Toppings (optional)

1 tomato or 10 cherry tomatoes

½ red (bell) pepper

100g (3½oz) button
mushrooms

¼ red or white onion

1 small courgette (zucchini)

10 pitted olives

75g (2½oz) mozzarella or
Cheddar cheese

1 teaspoon dried herbs
(oregano or basil), or 1
tablespoon fresh herbs

PIZZA

METHOD

1 Preheat the oven to 200°C/400°F/Gas mark 7.

2 Mix the flour, baking powder and salt in a large mixing bowl.

3 Make a well in the middle of the dry ingredients and add the yoghurt.

4 Use a butter knife to combine the ingredients until the dough starts
to come together.

5 Knead the dough lightly in the bowl, using your hand.

6 Grease two baking trays with oil and put them in the oven.

7 Lightly dust your work surface with flour. Divide the dough into 2
equal portions, and roll them both out to your desired shape until
about 5mm (¼ inch) thick.

8 Take the baking trays out of the oven with oven gloves and place
the rolled out dough onto the baking trays. Return to the oven for
3–4 minutes.

9 Prepare your chosen toppings: slice the tomatoes, pepper,
mushrooms, onion and courgette. Cut the olives in half and grate
the cheese.

10 Take the pizza bases out of the oven and flip them over with a fish slice.

11 Evenly spread 2 tablespoons of tomato purée onto each base.
Add your chosen toppings to the pizza. Sprinkle with dried herbs,
if using. Return the pizzas to the oven and cook for a further 10–12
minutes, or until crispy.

12 Sprinkle with fresh herbs, if using, to serve.

 You can put any toppings you like onto this pizza. If
you are using meat, it needs to be cooked first – good
ideas are ham, bacon or pepperoni. If you only have one
baking tray, you can cook the pizzas one at a time.

Photographed with tomatoes, pepper, mushrooms, red onion, courgette, olives and fresh basil

HOW TO: **HOW TO:**

LINING A   BAKING
FLAN TIN   BLIND
WITH PASTRY

INGREDIENTS

Flour, for rolling out

1 x quantity shortcrust pastry
(see page 178)
or 1 x 250g (9oz) packet of
shop-bought pastry

100ml (3½fl oz) milk

1 egg

Salt and pepper

1 small onion

2 or 3 of the following:
50g (1¾oz) mushrooms,
1 red (bell) pepper, 1 small
courgette (zucchini),
6 asparagus spears,
1 small leek

20g butter, or 1 tablespoon
olive oil

50g (1¾oz) Cheddar cheese

> The quiche can
> be eaten hot or
> cold, and served
> with a salad.

QUICHE

METHOD

1   Preheat the oven to 200°C/400°F/Gas mark 7 and get out a 22cm (8½ inch) flan tin (or a cake tin of the same diameter can work as an alternative).

2   Lightly dust the work surface with flour. Using a rolling pin, roll out the pastry to a large circle about 3mm (⅛ inch) thick all over, making it slightly bigger than your flan tin.

3   Use your pastry to line the flan tin, by rolling the pastry up on your rolling pin, then rolling it back out over your flan tin. Gently press it down into the edges of the tin. Trim the excess pastry off to neaten the edges. Place a circle of baking parchment over the top and cover it in baking beans. Cook in the oven for 7 minutes. Remove the baking beans and baking parchment and put the pastry back in the oven for 2 more minutes before taking it out of the oven. If you don't have baking beans, you can use rice instead.

4   Measure the milk in a measuring jug. Crack the egg into a bowl and beat it with a fork, then add it to the milk and mix. Add a pinch of salt and pepper.

5   Peel and chop the onion into small pieces on a chopping board. Slice or chop up the other two or three chosen vegetables into small pieces.

6   Heat the butter or oil in a frying pan on a medium heat and add the onion. Cook for about 2 minutes, stirring occasionally with a wooden spoon, until soft. Add the chopped vegetables and fry for a further 2 minutes, stirring until they also start to soften. Take the frying pan off the heat.

7   Spread the fried vegetables over the pastry base. Grate the cheese, then sprinkle over the top before pouring the liquid filling into the pastry case around the ingredients. Bake in the oven for a further 10–15 minutes or until it is set and golden brown.

 To make this richer, you can swap the milk for single (light) cream. You can also add other ingredients such as fried bacon strips, chopped ham or small broccoli florets.

Photographed with leek, courgette and mushroom

SPICY RICE

Serve with chopped fresh coriander (cilantro).

INGREDIENTS

1 tablespoon caster sugar

2 tablespoons mirin

2 tablespoons soy sauce

Black pepper

4 chicken breasts

440g (15½oz) long grain rice

2 onions

2 garlic cloves

5cm (2 inch) piece of fresh root ginger

2 tablespoons sesame oil

3 (bell) peppers (red/green/yellow)

2 chillies

200g (7oz) frozen peas

150g (5½oz) cashew nuts (optional)

150ml (5fl oz) teriyaki sauce

4 spring onions (scallions)

METHOD

1   In a mixing bowl, combine the sugar, mirin and soy sauce with a pinch of black pepper to create a marinade.

2   Cut the chicken breasts into chunks, add them to the marinade and stir in. Cover the bowl with cling film (plastic wrap) and leave it to marinate. Wash up thoroughly anything that has come into contact with the raw chicken, such as the chopping board and the knife.

3   Fill a saucepan half full with water and bring it to the boil. Put the rice in a sieve and rinse it under cold water before adding it to the saucepan of boiling water. Once the rice is boiling, lower the temperature to simmer. Leave the rice to cook for 12 minutes (or according to the instructions on the packet).

4   While the rice is cooking, peel and finely chop the onions, garlic and ginger. Add them to a wok or large frying pan with the sesame oil and fry for 1 minute on a medium heat.

5   Once the rice is cooked, drain it in a sieve and leave it to the side.

6   Wash and deseed the peppers and chillies. Chop the peppers into small cubes and finely chop the chillies, then add them both to the frying pan with the frozen peas.

7   In a separate pan, fry the marinated chicken on a medium heat for about 8 minutes, or until cooked all the way through and slightly caramelised.

8   Add the chicken to the large frying pan as well as the cashew nuts, if using, and stir through over a medium heat.

9   Lower the heat and add the cooked rice and teriyaki sauce, carefully folding it through until it is all combined.

10 Wash and finely chop the spring onions and stir them through.

11 Season with pepper to taste and bring off the heat.

   If you don't have a second frying pan, you can use a saucepan to fry the chicken. You can swap some of the ingredients to make this recipe quicker, such as pre-diced onions or microwaveable rice. However, the ginger is key to the flavour so make sure to use fresh root ginger.

Photographed with cashew nuts

Serves 4

 Suitable for freezing

 Saucepan with lid

This is delicious served with lamb or fish and new potatoes, or simply on pasta.

INGREDIENTS

3 tablespoons olive oil

1 onion

1 aubergine (eggplant)

1 garlic clove

1 red (bell) pepper

1 courgette (zucchini)

1 x 400g (14oz) can of chopped tomatoes

Salt and pepper

RATATOUILLE

METHOD

1   Pour the oil into a large saucepan (with a lid).

2   Peel the onion and chop it into small pieces, and add to the pan.

3   Cut the ends off the aubergine and chop it into 2cm (¾ inch) sized pieces. Add the aubergine to the pan and cook with the onion for 5 minutes on a medium heat, until the onion goes golden brown.

4   Peel and finely chop the garlic and add it to the pan.

5   Wash and deseed the pepper, then cut it into roughly 2cm (¾ inch) sized chunks and add them to pan.

6   Cut the ends off the courgette, then cut it into slices (roughly 1cm/½ inch thick) and add them to the pan too. Cook for a further 5 minutes, continuing on a medium heat, stirring occasionally until the courgette starts to go golden.

7   Add the tomatoes and stir. Place the lid on the pan and simmer on a low heat for approximately 20 minutes until the vegetables are tender and all the flavours are infused together. Stir occasionally so that it doesn't stick to the bottom of the pan.

8   Add salt and pepper to taste.

Serves 4

 Food processor OR Hand stick blender

Serve immediately, with a sprinkling of grated Parmesan on the top.

TAGLIATELLE WITH A PESTO SAUCE

INGREDIENTS

500g (1lb 2oz) fresh tagliatelle or 350g (12oz) dried pasta

50g (1¾oz) Parmesan cheese, plus extra grated Parmesan to serve

1 bunch of basil

1 garlic clove

4 tablespoons olive oil, plus extra if needed

50g (1¾oz) pine nuts

METHOD

1   Fill a saucepan with water and bring it to the boil on a high heat.

2   Put the pasta into the saucepan and bring the water back to the boil, then turn down to a medium-low heat to simmer for 4–5 minutes if fresh pasta, or 10–12 minutes if dried pasta (or for the time specified on the packet).

3   Grate the cheese.

4   Roughly chop the basil. Peel and chop the garlic.

5   Put the cheese, basil, garlic, olive oil and pine nuts into a food processor (or into a jug and use a hand stick blender) and blitz the ingredients into a thick pesto sauce. If the pesto is too thick, add a little more oil to 'thin' down – this will depend on how big the bunch of basil is.

6   Remove the pasta from the heat and drain it in a colander over the sink. Tip the pasta back into the saucepan.

7   Pour the pesto sauce over the pasta and mix through.

 For a creamy chicken pesto pasta, you can fry thin strips of chicken breast in a frying pan with oil until cooked. At step 7, add the cooked chicken and 200ml (7fl oz) single (light) cream to the saucepan and stir together.

Serves 4

Serve immediately, while hot.

RISOTTO

INGREDIENTS

1 onion

350g (12oz) button
   mushrooms

2 tablespoons olive oil

25g (1oz) butter

350g (12oz) arborio rice

1.5 litres vegetable stock
   (made with 2 stock cubes
   and boiling water)

1 small courgette (zucchini)

125g (4½oz) asparagus tips

100g (3½oz) fresh or frozen
   broad beans or peas

Salt and pepper

50g (1¾oz) Parmesan cheese

METHOD

1   Peel and chop the onion.

2   Wash and slice the mushrooms.

3   Using a large frying pan or wok, fry the onion in the oil and butter
    on a low heat until soft – about 3 minutes. Add the mushrooms and
    cook for a further 3 minutes.

4   Add the rice to the pan and stir thoroughly with a wooden spoon,
    then turn up the heat to medium.

5   Add about 250ml (9fl oz) of the stock and stir until all the liquid
    is absorbed. Add the remaining stock, 250ml (9fl oz) at a time,
    repeating this process. Continue until all the stock has been added
    and the rice is nearly cooked – this will take about 20 minutes.

6   While the rice is cooking, wash and slice the courgette thinly and
    cut the asparagus into 2cm (¾ inch) sized pieces.

7   Add the courgette, asparagus and broad beans or peas to the rice,
    and cook, stirring continuously for a further 5 minutes.

8   Season with salt and pepper to taste.

9   Remove the risotto from the heat and grate the Parmesan cheese
    over the top.

   You need to stir risotto constantly while cooking,
       otherwise it sticks to the pan. You can adapt this recipe
       by adding different vegetables, or by adding a packet
       of cooked mixed seafood at step 6 (using fish stock
       instead of vegetable stock).

4 Serves 4

 Suitable for freezing

 Hand stick blender

This is the perfect salad for a barbecue. Serve cold.

SUMMER NOODLE SALAD

METHOD

1 Wash and finely slice the carrots, radishes, spring onions and sugar snaps and put them into a large mixing bowl.

2 Bring a large pan of water to the boil and cook the noodles as directed on the packaging. Drain and rinse them in cold water before adding them to the mixing bowl. (Alternatively, you can use fresh noodles that don't require cooking and add them straight to the salad.)

3 Peel and chop the garlic and the ginger into small pieces.

4 Put all the dressing ingredients into a measuring jug and blitz together using a hand stick blender for about 30 seconds, or until smooth.

5 Add the dressing to the mixing bowl and toss through.

6 Wash and chop the coriander leaves and mix through the salad.

 You can swap the egg noodles for courgette (zucchini) spaghetti/spiralised courgette. If you don't have groundnut oil, use olive oil. However, the sesame oil is important for the flavour.

INGREDIENTS

For the salad

4 baby carrots

6 radishes

4 spring onions (scallions)

50–75g sugar snap peas

250g (9oz) egg noodles

½ bunch fresh coriander (cilantro) leaves

For the dressing

1 garlic clove

2.5cm (1 inch) piece of fresh root ginger

3 tablespoons red or white wine vinegar

2 tablespoons soy sauce

2 tablespoons sesame oil

4 tablespoons groundnut oil

1 tablespoon caster sugar

Salt and pepper

This dish can be eaten warm or cold. Serve with a sprinkle of freshly grated Parmesan if you wish.

PASTA SALAD

METHOD

1 Fill a saucepan half-full with water and put over a high heat. When the water starts to boil, add the pasta and lower the heat to simmer. Follow the instructions on the packet to see how long it takes to cook (usually 10–12 minutes, depending on the type of pasta).

2 While the pasta is cooking, peel the onion and chop into thin slices. Wash and cut the ends off the courgettes, then cut them into slices. Peel and finely chop the garlic.

3 When the pasta is cooked, drain it into a colander over the sink.

4 Put the olive oil in a saucepan and fry the onion, courgette and garlic for 5 minutes, or until soft. Cut the tomatoes in half and add to the pan, then cook for a further 2 minutes.

5 Put the drained pasta into a bowl. Carefully pour the vegetables over the pasta and gently mix together. Tear up the basil leaves and add them to the dish.

INGREDIENTS

400g (14oz) pasta (or whole-wheat pasta, if preferred)

1 red onion

2 courgettes (zucchini)

2 garlic cloves

3 tablespoons olive oil

400g (14oz) cherry tomatoes (about 12)

Handful of fresh basil leaves

4   Serves 4

Hand stick blender

SUMMER PLATTER
WITH BURRATA OR STEAK

INGREDIENTS

For the salad

½ butternut squash

2 sweet potatoes

2 tablespoons olive oil

2 teaspoons honey

1 teaspoon chilli flakes

1 tablespoon oil, for frying
steak (if using)

4 fillet steaks or 2 balls burrata

1 bag rocket (arugula) leaves
(about 120g/4¼oz)

100g (3½oz) pomegranate
seeds (optional)

10g (⅓oz) micro leaves
(optional)

METHOD

1   Preheat the oven to 180°C/350°F/Gas mark 6.

2   Peel and chop the butternut squash into 2cm (¾ inch) slices. Wash the sweet potatoes (you can either peel them or leave the skin on) and cut them into 2cm (¾ inch) cubes. Spread them both out on a baking tray and pour the oil and honey over. Sprinkle the chilli flakes on the top. Toss together with your hands until it is all mixed together and the vegetables are coated in the oil.

3   Put the baking tray in the oven and cook the vegetables for 45–50 minutes until soft and golden.

4   Roughly chop the parsley, mint and basil and put it into a jug. Peel and chop the garlic and add it to the jug with all the other salsa verde ingredients. Use a hand stick blender and blitz the ingredients into a thick sauce.

5   If you are using fillet steaks, fry them with the oil in a frying pan over a high heat. The length of time will depend on the thickness of the meat, and how you like it cooked (see tip overleaf). Alternatively, you can barbecue the meat.

6   Once the meat is cooked, leave it on a chopping board to 'rest' for 10 minutes, covered with foil.

7   Take the butternut squash and sweet potatoes out of the oven with oven gloves.

Photographed with burrata and sprinkled with pomegranate and Amaranth micro leaf

Photographed with fillet steak and sprinkled with pomegranate and Amaranth micro leaf

For the salsa verde

1 small bunch of parsley

1 small bunch of mint

1 small bunch of basil

1 garlic clove

1 tablespoon red wine
 vinegar

4 tablespoons olive oil

1 teaspoon caster sugar

Salt and pepper

Serve immediately.

8 Spread out the rocket leaves on a platter or a large plate, then spread the sweet potato and squash on top. Break up the burrata if using and spread over the vegetables. If using meat, slice the steak thinly and spread it out over the vegetables.

9 Spoon the salsa verde over the top of the whole dish. If using, sprinkle the dish with pomegranate seeds and micro leaves.

 This is for a special occasion, as fillet steak is expensive. Try it with cheaper cuts of steak, grilled lamb or chicken instead.

Approximate times for cooking steak:

Rare – 2 minutes each side
Medium – 4 minutes each side
Well Done – 6 minutes each side

2 Serves 2

 Suitable for freezing

Serve two toad in the holes per person with boiled vegetables such as broccoli and carrots.

INGREDIENTS

Oil, for greasing

4 large sausages or
8 cocktail sausages

75g (2½oz) plain
(all-purpose) flour

1 egg

200ml (7fl oz) milk

4 sprigs of rosemary
(optional)

For the onion gravy

1 onion

1 tablespoon oil

1 stock cube (beef,
chicken or vegetable)

250ml (9fl oz) boiling water

1 teaspoon sugar

TOAD IN THE HOLE

METHOD

1   Preheat the oven to 220°C/425°F/Gas mark 8. Brush a small roasting tin or 4-hole Yorkshire pudding tray with oil and add the sausages. Cook in the oven for 10 minutes if using large sausages, or 5 minutes if using small sausages.

2   Put the flour in a mixing bowl and make a well in the centre. Break the egg into a separate bowl (make sure there is no shell), then pour it into the flour well.

3   Add about half the milk and beat the mixture using a whisk until it is smooth and lump-free. Add the remaining milk and whisk in.

4   Take the baking tray of sausages out of the oven with oven gloves and pour the batter mixture evenly over the sausages. Scatter the rosemary sprigs over the top, if using.

5   Carefully place the tin back into the oven and cook for a further 15–20 minutes until the batter is puffed up and golden.

6   While the toad in the hole is cooking, make the onion gravy. Peel and slice the onion. Put the onion and oil in a small saucepan on a medium heat, and fry until the onion is golden brown and caramelising.

7   Put the stock cube in a measuring jug and add the boiling water. Stir until the stock cube has dissolved. Add the stock and the sugar to the onion in the saucepan and boil on a high heat for 2 minutes until reduced (thickened) slightly.

 If you don't have a 4-hole tray, use a small roasting tin and make one large toad in the hole rather than individual ones. Divide it into two portions to serve.

Photographed with rosemary

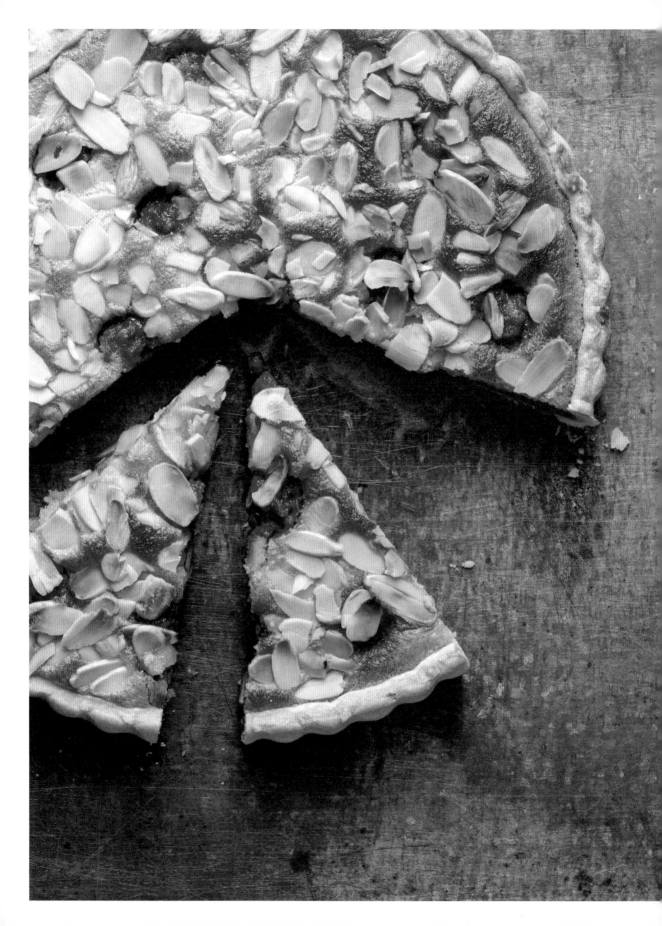

DESSERTS

HOW TO:
LINING A
FLAN TIN
WITH PASTRY

HOW TO:
SEPARATING
EGGS

LEMON MERINGUE PIE

INGREDIENTS

For the base and filling

Flour, for rolling out

1 x quantity shortcrust pastry
(see page 178) or
250g (9oz) bought
shortcrust pastry

2 lemons

150g (5½oz) caster sugar

3 tablespoons cornflour
(cornstarch)

150ml (5fl oz) water

3 egg yolks

For the meringue topping

3 egg whites

150g (5½oz) caster sugar

METHOD

1   Preheat the oven to 200°C/400°F/Gas mark 7 and get out a 22cm (8½ inch) flan tin (or a cake tin of the same diameter).

2   Lightly dust the work surface with flour. Using a rolling pin, roll out the pastry to a large circle about 3mm (⅛ inch) thick all over, making it slightly bigger than your flan tin.

3   Use your pastry to line the flan tin, by rolling the pastry up on your rolling pin, then rolling it back out over your flan tin. Gently press it down into the edges of the tin. Trim the excess pastry off to neaten the edges. Place a circle of baking parchment over the top and cover it in baking beans. Cook in the oven for 7 minutes. Remove the baking beans and baking parchment and put the pastry back in the oven for 2 more minutes before taking it out of the oven.

4   Zest the lemons, then squeeze the juice from them. Put the zest and juice into a small saucepan with the caster sugar, cornflour and water. Stir the mixture until the cornflour is mixed in and dissolved. Place the saucepan over a low heat and stir continuously until the mixture boils and thickens. Take the saucepan off the heat and leave it to cool.

5   Separate the eggs one at a time, making sure you don't get any yolk into the white. Keep the whites for the meringues in a separate, clean large bowl. Beat the egg yolks into the cooled lemon sauce filling (it will become scrambled if the mixture isn't cool). Pour the lemon sauce into the pastry case.

6   To make the meringue topping, whisk the egg whites in a large bowl until they are stiff, either with an electric hand mixer or a balloon whisk. Add in 1 tablespoon of sugar at a time, continuing to whisk, until all the sugar is used up.

7   Spoon or pipe the meringue over the lemon filling, then bake for a further 10–15 minutes, until the meringue is a light golden colour.

 You can make this with any citrus fruit – try using limes or oranges instead.

HOW TO: **HOW TO:**

PEELING AND CORING APPLES | RUBBING IN METHOD

INGREDIENTS

For the base and filling

400g (14oz) cooking apples (about 2 large or 3 small)

25g (1oz) sugar

2 tablespoons water

1 teaspoon ground cinnamon (optional)

150g (5½oz) blackberries (optional)

For the crumble

75g (2½oz) butter or block margarine

150g (5½oz) plain (all-purpose) flour

75g (2½oz) sugar

50g (1¾oz) oats

Serve hot with single (light) cream, vanilla ice cream or custard.

FRUIT CRUMBLE

METHOD

1 Preheat the oven to 180°C/350°F/Gas mark 6.

2 Peel, core and chop the apples. Put the apples in a microwaveable bowl and sprinkle with the 25g (1oz) sugar and 2 tablespoons water.

3 Put the bowl into the microwave for 3 minutes on high power. This semi-cooks the fruit. Be careful taking it out of the microwave as the bowl will be hot. (Alternatively, you can boil the apples, sugar and water in a small saucepan for 3 minutes on a medium heat, stirring occasionally.)

4 Add the cinnamon and blackberries to the apples (if using) and mix in. Pour the mixture into an ovenproof dish.

5 To make the crumble, cut the butter or margarine into small pieces with a butter knife. Put the flour into a large mixing bowl and add the butter. Use your fingertips to rub the butter into the flour so that it looks like breadcrumbs.

6 Add the sugar and mix it in, then mix in the oats.

7 Spoon the crumble mixture evenly over the fruit but do not push it down.

8 Place the dish on a baking tray and cook it in the oven for about 20 minutes until golden brown.

 You can swap the cooking apples for 300g (10½oz) chopped plums, gooseberries, rhubarb, or a combination of them. If using margarine, it must be block margarine, not spreadable.

Photographed with apple and blackberries

4 Serves 4

 Suitable for freezing

HOW TO: PEELING AND CORING APPLES

HOW TO: MAKING AN APPLE STRUDEL

APPLE STRUDEL

INGREDIENTS

400g (14oz) cooking apples (about 2 large or 3 small)

Juice of ½ lemon (or 1 tablespoon bottled lemon juice)

75g (2½oz) demerara sugar (or caster sugar)

25g (1oz) fresh breadcrumbs

50g (1¾oz) sultanas (golden raisins)

1 teaspoon ground cinnamon

50g (1¾oz) butter

3 or 4 sheets filo (phyllo) pastry (fresh or defrosted)

Icing (confectioners') sugar, for dusting

Serve hot or cold with custard, cream or vanilla ice cream.

METHOD

1   Preheat the oven to 200°C/400°F/Gas mark 7.

2   Peel, core and chop the apples and put them into a mixing bowl.

3   Add the lemon juice, sugar, breadcrumbs, sultanas and cinnamon and mix together.

4   Melt the butter either in a small (microwaveable) bowl in the microwave or in a small saucepan over a low heat. Lightly grease a baking tray with a little of the melted butter.

5   Open the packet of filo, remove the sheets of pastry, and cover with a clean, damp cloth to stop them drying out. Unfold one sheet of filo pastry at a time, laying it out horizontally on a work surface. Brush the pastry liberally with melted butter. Then add the next sheet one-third of the way up and brush with butter. Repeat this with the third and fourth sheets of filo.

6   Place the apple filling onto the pastry about one-third of the way up the sheet, arranging it in a long pile across the width of the pastry and leaving about 3cm (1¼ inch) of pastry each side without any filling on. Roll the pastry up, over the filling, three-quarters of the way up. Then brush the two side edges and the top edge with more butter, 'gluing' it together. Fold in the side edges and roll the rest of the way up.

7   Place the strudel on a large baking tray with the join on the underside.

8   Brush the strudel with the remaining melted butter, then bake it for about 20 minutes or until golden brown and crisp.

9   Remove it from the baking tray immediately (so that it doesn't stick) and place the strudel on a serving dish or plate. Dust with icing sugar just before serving.

Serves 8 (makes
1 large or 8 individual
cheesecakes)

 Electric hand mixer

You can
decorate this
with most fruits.

INGREDIENTS

150g (5½oz) gingernut
biscuits or digestives

¾ teaspoon ground
cinnamon

¾ teaspoon ground nutmeg

40g (1½oz) caster sugar

2 lemons

100g (3½oz) butter

300ml (10½fl oz) double
(heavy) cream

320g (11¼oz) cream cheese

1 can condensed milk
(approx. 397g/14oz)

300g (10½oz) mixed
strawberries, blueberries
and raspberries to decorate
(optional)

CHEESECAKE

METHOD

1   Get out a deep, 20cm (8 inch) loose-bottomed cake tin to make
    1 large cheesecake, or 8 ramekin pots or glasses to make 8 individual
    cheesecakes.

2   Crush the biscuits in a bowl using the end of a rolling pin, until they are
    crumbs. Add the cinnamon, nutmeg and sugar.

3   Zest the lemons using the finest holes on a grater, taking off just the
    yellow outer skin. You should end up with about 2 teaspoons of zest.
    Add this to the bowl and mix the ingredients together.

4   Melt the butter in a small (microwaveable) bowl in the microwave for
    about 30 seconds (or in a small saucepan over a low heat), then pour
    it over the biscuit mixture. Mix it all together.

5   Tip the biscuit mixture into your tin, or put one-eighth of the mixture
    into the bottom of each ramekin pot or glass. Press the base down
    with a fork and put it into the fridge to set. While the base is chilling,
    make the filling.

6   Cut the lemons in half and squeeze the juice out.

7   Put the cream into a large bowl and, using the electric hand mixer,
    whisk until it thickens and forms soft peaks. Add the cream cheese,
    condensed milk and lemon juice and whisk it together so that there
    are no lumps. Pour the mixture over the biscuit base or spoon the
    mixture equally over the individual bases.

8   Keep in the fridge until ready to serve.

9   Before serving, wash and dry the mixed berries (if using) and
    decorate the top of the cheesecake.

   This is a no-bake recipe. An electric hand mixer is a lot
    easier to use than a balloon whisk.

Photographed with a topping of strawberries, blueberries and raspberries

HOW TO: **HOW TO:**

LINING A   BAKING
FLAN TIN   BLIND
WITH PASTRY

BAKEWELL TART

INGREDIENTS

Flour, for rolling out

1 x quantity shortcrust pastry
(see page 178) or 250g (9oz)
shop-bought shortcrust
pastry

4 heaped tablespoons
raspberry jam

100g (3½oz) raspberries

3 eggs

75g (2½oz) butter

75g (2½oz) caster sugar

1 teaspoon vanilla extract

75g (2½oz) ground almonds

25g (1oz) flaked (sliced)
almonds (optional)

METHOD

1 Preheat the oven to 200°C/400°F/Gas mark 7 and get out a 22cm (8½ inch) flan tin (or a cake tin of the same diameter can work as an alternative).

2 Lightly dust the work surface with flour. Using a rolling pin, roll out the pastry to a large circle about 3mm (⅛ inch) thick all over, making it slightly bigger than your flan tin.

3 Use your pastry to line the flan tin, by rolling the pastry up on your rolling pin, then rolling it back out over your flan tin. Gently press it down into the edges of the tin. Trim the excess pastry off to neaten the edges. Place a circle of baking parchment over the top and cover it in baking beans. Cook in the oven for 7 minutes. Remove the baking beans and baking parchment and put the pastry back in the oven for 2 more minutes before taking it out of the oven. If you don't have baking beans, you can use rice instead.

4 Turn the oven down to 190°C/375°F/Gas mark 6.

5 Spread the raspberry jam evenly over the pastry base. Scatter the raspberries evenly over the jam.

6 Crack the eggs into a mixing bowl and beat them with a fork.

7 Melt the butter in a small (microwaveable) bowl in the microwave for about 30 seconds (or in a small saucepan over a low heat).

8 Add the melted butter, sugar, vanilla extract and ground almonds to the eggs in the mixing bowl.

9 Pour the mixture over the jam and raspberries, and sprinkle the flaked almonds over the top, if using.

10 Bake in the oven for 25–30 minutes until firm in the middle.

 You can use any flavour of jam or marmalade that you like.

Serve warm with crème fraîche.

Photographed with flaked almonds on top

Serves 6

 Blow torch/grill

 6 ramekin dishes or ovenproof dishes

CRÈME BRÛLÉE

INGREDIENTS

1 vanilla pod

140g (5oz) caster sugar

500ml (17fl oz) double (heavy) cream

3 large eggs

6 tablespoons demerara sugar

METHOD

1   Cut the vanilla pod in half lengthways. Scrape the tiny seeds into a small saucepan, then put the rest of the vanilla pod in too.

2   Add the sugar and cream to the pan, put it over a medium heat and bring to a simmer for 1 minute. Remove the saucepan from the heat.

3   Crack the eggs into a mixing bowl and whisk.

4   Place a sieve over the mixing bowl and pour the vanilla cream mixture from the saucepan, through the sieve. Discard the vanilla pod from the sieve. Whisk the eggs and cream together, then pour the mixture back into the saucepan.

5   Cook the cream mixture on a low heat and stir continuously with a balloon whisk for about 4 minutes, or until it starts to thicken. As soon as it starts to thicken, take it off the heat and pour it into 6 shallow ovenproof dishes/ramekins. Leave them to cool in the fridge for at least 45 minutes.

6   Just before serving, sprinkle a tablespoon of demerara sugar over the top of the cooled set cream. Use either a kitchen blow torch to melt the sugar and turn it into caramel, or place the dishes under the grill (broiler) on a high heat until the sugar starts to melt and bubble. Keep an eye on them under the grill as the sugar can burn quickly.

7   Serve immediately – be careful as the pot will be hot.

 Delicious with a few raspberries, blackberries or stewed rhubarb in the bottom of the crème brûlée. Place 1 tablespoon of the fruit in each ramekin dish at the start of step 5, before pouring over the vanilla cream mixture.

Photographed with stewed rhubarb

Serves 4

 Suitable for freezing

Serve hot with
vanilla ice cream.

FRUIT TARTS

METHOD

1 Preheat the oven to 200°C/400°F/Gas mark 7 and get out a baking tray.

2 Lightly dust a work surface with flour and roll out the pastry into a rectangle about 3mm (⅛ inch) thick and measuring about 30 x 20cm (12 x 8 inch). Cut it in half widthways, making two 15 x 20cm (6 x 8 inch) pieces. Place the two pieces of pastry onto the baking tray and score a 1cm (½ inch) border all the way around the edges, being careful not to cut through the pastry.

3 Spread the jam over the middle section of both the pastry pieces, making sure you stay inside the border.

4 Cut the fruit in half and remove the stones. Then slice the fruit into even thin slices.

5 Arrange the fruit on top of the jam neatly.

6 Put the butter in a microwaveable bowl and melt it in the microwave for about 20 seconds, then brush the fruit with the melted butter. Sprinkle the sugar over the top.

7 Place the tarts in the oven and bake for 15 minutes, or until golden brown.

 You can use other types of jam if you prefer and different types of firm fruit – cooking apples, nectarines or pears would work well.

INGREDIENTS

Flour, for rolling out

½ x quantity rough puff pastry (see page 176) or 250g (9oz) shop-bought puff pastry

2 tablespoons strawberry or raspberry jam

4–6 plums or apricots

10g (⅓oz) butter

1 tablespoon caster sugar

Photographed with plums

Serves 4

 Suitable for freezing

 Electric hand mixer

HOW TO:

**TURNING
OUT CAKES**

PINEAPPLE UPSIDE DOWN CAKE

INGREDIENTS

Butter or vegetable oil, for greasing

1 tablespoon brown or demerara sugar (or 2 tablespoons golden syrup)

1 small can of pineapple rings

4 raspberries or 4 glacé cherries (optional)

100g (3½oz) butter or block margarine

100g (3½oz) caster sugar

2 eggs

100g (3½oz) self-raising flour

Serve warm with single (light) cream or crème fraîche.

METHOD

1 Preheat the oven to 180°C/350°F/Gas mark 6. Grease a 22cm (8½ inch) round cake tin with a little butter or oil and line the base with a circle of baking parchment.

2 Sprinkle the brown or demerara sugar over the base of the tin evenly, or drizzle the golden syrup over if using instead.

3 Drain the pineapple rings using a sieve. Put 4 rings of pineapple on top of the brown sugar and, if using, place a raspberry or glacé cherry inside each hole of the pineapple rings.

4 Put the butter or margarine into a mixing bowl. Make sure it is soft enough to mix easily. If it is not, put it into the microwave in a microwaveable bowl for 10–20 seconds to soften (but not melt!).

5 Add the caster sugar to the butter and beat together with a wooden spoon or electric hand mixer until creamy.

6 Add the eggs one at a time and beat in.

7 Add the flour and mix it in gently.

8 Pour the cake mixture over the pineapple rings and spread it out evenly and carefully, so as not to move the fruit. Put the cake in the oven for 20–25 minutes until golden brown.

9 Allow it to cool in the tin for 2 minutes, then run a knife around the side of the tin to loosen the sponge. Put a serving plate over the top of the tin and carefully turn the cake upside down. Remove the tin and peel off the baking parchment to reveal the fruit pattern and syrup.

 You can use any 'firm' canned fruit instead of pineapple; peaches, pears or apricots work well. Remember when arranging the fruit that it will be visible when you turn out your cake, so try and keep it neat!

PANCAKES

For sweet toppings, try lemon juice and icing sugar or fresh fruit. For savoury toppings, try ham and grated cheese.

INGREDIENTS

100g (3½oz) plain (all-purpose) flour

1 egg

250ml (9fl oz) milk

2 tablespoons oil

METHOD

1 Put the flour in a bowl and make a well in the centre.

2 Break the egg into a cup (and make sure there is no shell), then pour it into the well in the flour.

3 Add 100ml (3½fl oz) of the milk and beat the mixture with a whisk until smooth.

4 Add the rest of the milk and whisk thoroughly. Pour the batter into a jug.

5 Heat a teaspoon of the oil in a small frying pan on a high heat, then pour in enough batter to thinly coat the base of the pan. You may need to swirl the pan around to get the batter to spread out and coat the whole base.

6 Cook for about 1½ minutes, or until the underneath is golden brown. Flip the pancakes using a fish slice or palette knife and cook on the other side for about 30 seconds until it is lightly golden.

7 Slide the pancake onto a plate and repeat to cook the remaining batter, adding a little more oil to the frying pan each time.

 You can check if the pancake is 'done' underneath by lifting the edge of the pancake using a fish slice or palette knife and taking a look.

Photographed with lemon and sugar

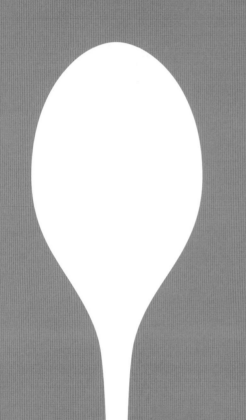

BAKING

Makes 8 biscuits

 Suitable for freezing

 Food processor (optional)

HOW TO:

RUBBING IN METHOD

INGREDIENTS

Butter or vegetable oil, for greasing

100g (3½oz) butter (cold from the fridge)

150g (5½oz) plain (all-purpose) flour, plus extra for dusting

50g (1¾oz) caster sugar, plus 2–3 tablespoons extra for sprinkling

SHORTBREAD BISCUITS

METHOD

1 Preheat the oven to 160°C/315°F/Gas mark 4. Lightly grease a baking tray with a little butter or oil.

2 Cut the butter into small cubes, before adding it to a large mixing bowl along with the flour and sugar. Using the rubbing in method, rub the butter into the flour and sugar using your fingertips until it looks like breadcrumbs. Use your hands to combine the mixture into a ball of dough. (Alternatively, put the butter, flour and sugar into a food processor and mix until the dough starts to stick together.)

3 On a lightly floured surface, use a rolling pin to gently roll the dough out until it is about 5mm (¼ inch) thick. This is a very 'crumbly' mixture, so keep pressing the edges in with the sides of your hands as you roll to keep it neat.

4 Using a sharp knife, cut the dough into 8 rectangles, or make 8 circles using a cookie cutter, and carefully transfer them to the baking tray. Prick them all over with a fork for decoration.

5 Bake them for 10–15 minutes or until they are a pale golden brown colour. Remove the tray from the oven using oven gloves.

6 Leave them on the tray for 2 minutes to harden, then sprinkle them with the extra sugar. Carefully lift the biscuits onto a wire rack using a fish slice or palette knife.

Makes about 20 biscuits

 Suitable for freezing (without the chocolate)

HOW TO:

SEPARATING EGGS

VANILLA & ALMOND BISCUITS

INGREDIENTS

Butter or vegetable oil, for greasing (optional)

210g (7½oz) butter

70g (2½oz) caster sugar (plus an extra 3 teaspoons if not using chocolate)

1 teaspoon vanilla extract

1 egg yolk

100g (3½oz) ground almonds

250g (9oz) plain (all-purpose) flour, plus extra for dusting

100g (3½oz) dark (bittersweet) chocolate (optional)

METHOD

1   Preheat the oven to 170°C/325°F/Gas mark 5. Lightly grease a baking tray with a little butter or oil, or line it with baking parchment.

2   Put the butter into a mixing bowl. Make sure it is soft enough to mix easily. If it is not, put it into the microwave in a microwaveable bowl for 10–20 seconds to soften (but not melt!).

3   Add the caster sugar to the butter and beat together with a wooden spoon until creamy. Add the vanilla extract. Separate the white from the yolk of your egg, and add just the yolk. Add the ground almonds and flour and mix together.

4   Dust your hands with a bit of flour and roll a small amount (about 1 heaped teaspoon) of the mixture into a ball shape. Place the ball onto the baking tray, then press down lightly with a fork to flatten slightly. Repeat this step to use up all of the dough and make about 20 biscuits.

5   Cook the biscuits for about 15 minutes until pale golden around the edges. Remove them from the oven and leave them to cool for 5 minutes on the tray, then lift them onto a wire rack to cool completely.

6   If you aren't using chocolate to decorate, sprinkle the additional 3 teaspoons of caster sugar over the biscuits at this stage. If you are adding chocolate, break the chocolate into small pieces and put it into a small microwaveable bowl. Put it into the microwave for 20 seconds, then stir and return to the microwave for 20 seconds. Repeat until the chocolate is melted and runny. (Alternatively, melt the chocolate in a heatproof bowl over a small saucepan of water over a low heat.) Dip the biscuits halfway into the melted chocolate, then leave them to set on a sheet of baking parchment.

 You can use the leftover egg white to make mini meringues: whisk the egg white into firm peaks, adding 50g (1¾oz) caster sugar, a little at a time, as you whisk. Put heaped teaspoons onto a lined baking tray. Bake them in the oven at 120°C/250°F/Gas mark 1 for 40 minutes.

Photographed dipped in dark chocolate

Serves 8

 Suitable for freezing

HOW TO:

TURNING
OUT CAKES

CARROT CAKE

INGREDIENTS

For the cake

Butter or vegetable oil,
for greasing

175g (6oz) plain wholemeal
flour

175g (6oz) soft brown sugar

1 teaspoon ground cinnamon

1 teaspoon bicarbonate of
soda (baking soda)

1 large carrot (about 175g/6oz)

175ml (5½fl oz) vegetable oil

2 eggs

For the topping

25g (1oz) butter (at room
temperature)

50g (1¾oz) cream cheese

150g (5½oz) icing
(confectioners') sugar

1 tablespoon milk

1 tablespoon chopped
walnuts (optional)

METHOD

1   Preheat the oven to 170°C/325°F/Gas mark 5. Grease a 20cm (8 inch) round cake tin and line it with a circle of baking parchment (or put 8 muffin cases into a muffin tin).

2   Put the flour, sugar, cinnamon and bicarbonate of soda into a large mixing bowl and mix them together.

3   Peel and grate the carrot, add it to the mixing bowl and stir.

4   Measure the oil into a measuring jug. Crack the eggs one at a time and add them to the oil. Beat them together with a fork.

5   Pour the oil mixture into the mixing bowl and stir all the ingredients together.

6   Pour the mixture into the prepared tin and spread it out evenly. Bake for 30 minutes until firm to the touch. (Alternatively, spoon the mixture evenly into the muffin cases and bake them for about 15 minutes, or until risen.)

7   Leave the cake(s) to cool for 5 minutes in the tin, then turn out onto a wire rack and wait until fully cool before icing.

8   To make the icing, beat the butter, cream cheese, icing sugar and milk together in a large mixing bowl, until smooth and creamy.

9   Spread the icing evenly on the top of the cake. Decorate with the chopped walnuts, if using.

 For a more textured cake, try adding 50g (1¾oz) of chopped walnuts at the end of step 3. You can double the quantity of cake mixture and icing mixture to make 2 cakes, then sandwich them together with the icing (as shown in the photo), which will serve 16 people.

Photographed using 2 cakes, with icing and chopped walnuts

Makes 12 brownies

 Suitable for freezing

 Electric hand mixer

BROWNIES

INGREDIENTS

Butter or vegetable oil,
for greasing

190g (6¾oz) dark
(bittersweet) chocolate

190g (6¾oz) salted butter

3 large eggs

250g (9oz) caster sugar

2 teaspoons vanilla extract

115g (4oz) plain (all-purpose)
flour

150g (5½oz) chopped
walnuts (optional)

METHOD

1   Preheat the oven to 180°C/350°F/Gas mark 6. Line a rectangular tin (about 26 x 20cm/10½ x 8 inch) with baking parchment and grease with butter or a little oil.

2   Break up the chocolate into small pieces and put it into a small saucepan. Add the butter and melt them together in the saucepan over a low heat, stirring continuously until there are no lumps. Turn off the heat and leave the mixture to cool for 5 minutes.

3   Crack the eggs separately to make sure there is no shell in them, and put them into a large mixing bowl with the sugar and vanilla extract. Beat together with an electric hand mixer or wooden spoon until combined. Add the cooled chocolate mixture and mix them together.

4   Add the flour and the nuts (if using) and fold in all the ingredients with a metal spoon.

5   Pour the mixture into the prepared tin and bake it for about 25 minutes. The top should have a slightly cracked crust.

6   Remove the tin from the oven and score the brownies into 12 squares with a sharp knife. Leave them to cool before cutting and removing them from the tin. The top and bottom should be firm but the middle should still be gooey.

You can make 'blondies' by replacing the dark chocolate with white chocolate and mixing in 100g (3½oz) extra white chocolate chunks at the end of step 3.

Serves 8

 Suitable for freezing

 Electric hand mixer

HOW TO:

TURNING
OUT CAKES

INGREDIENTS

Butter or vegetable oil,
  for greasing

100g (3½oz) butter or
  margarine

140g (5oz) caster sugar,
  plus an extra 1 teaspoon
  for sprinkling

3 eggs

1 teaspoon vanilla extract

50g (1¾oz) plain
  (all-purpose) flour

75g (2½oz) ground almonds

1 tablespoon flaked almonds
  (optional)

Serve with
crème fraîche
and raspberries,
as in the
picture.

ALMOND CAKE

METHOD

1 Preheat the oven to 170°C/325°F/Gas mark 5. Grease a 20cm (8 inch) round cake tin with a little oil or butter and line the base with a circle of baking parchment.

2 Put the butter or margarine into a mixing bowl. Make sure it is soft enough to mix easily. If it is not, put it into the microwave in a microwaveable bowl for 10–20 seconds to soften (but not melt!).

3 Add the caster sugar to the butter and beat together with a wooden spoon or electric hand mixer until creamy.

4 Add the eggs one at a time, cracking them into a separate bowl to make sure there is no shell in them, then adding them to the mixing bowl. Add the vanilla extract and mix in.

5 Fold in the flour and ground almonds with a metal spoon.

6 Pour the mixture into the prepared tin and spread it out evenly. Sprinkle the flaked almonds over the top, if using.

7 Put the cake into the oven and bake for about 25 minutes until light golden brown.

8 Turn the cake out onto a wire rack, then turn it back over. Sprinkle it with a teaspoon of caster sugar and leave it to cool.

Makes 12 muffins

 Suitable for freezing

HOW TO:

PEELING AND CORING APPLES

APPLE, BLUEBERRY & CINNAMON MUFFINS

INGREDIENTS

300g (10½oz) plain (all-purpose) flour

2 teaspoons baking powder

2 teaspoons ground cinnamon

200g (7oz) caster sugar

225ml (8fl oz) milk

1 egg

1 teaspoon vanilla extract

50g (1¾oz) butter or margarine

1 cooking apple

100g (3½oz) blueberries

METHOD

1 Preheat the oven to 180°C/350°F/Gas mark 6. Put 12 muffin cases into a muffin tin.

2 Put the flour, baking powder, cinnamon and sugar into a large mixing bowl and mix them together using a metal spoon.

3 Pour the milk into a measuring jug.

4 Crack the egg into a cup, making sure there is no shell in it, then add it to the milk in the measuring jug. Whisk with a fork, then add the vanilla extract and mix it in.

5 Melt the butter in a small microwaveable bowl in the microwave for about 30 seconds, or in a small saucepan on a low heat. Add this to the jug and stir.

6 Pour the liquid mixture into the dry mixture and fold in using the metal spoon.

7 Peel, core and chop the apple into small pieces and add them to your muffin mixture. Wash the blueberries in a sieve, then add them to the mixture and stir in.

8 Spoon the mixture evenly into the muffin cases using a metal spoon (filling them about three-quarters of the way up) and bake in the oven for 25–30 minutes until they are golden brown. Leave to cool slightly before serving.

 If you prefer, you can swap the blueberries for raspberries or blackberries.

Makes about 6 biscuits

 Suitable for freezing

HOW TO:
MAKING A PIPING BAG

INGREDIENTS

Butter or vegetable oil, for greasing

50g (1¾oz) butter or margarine

25g (1oz) brown sugar

75g (2½oz) golden syrup (light corn syrup)

1 teaspoon ground ginger

125g plain (all-purpose) flour, plus extra for dusting

½ teaspoon bicarbonate of soda (baking soda)

For the icing (optional)

50g (1¾oz) icing (confectioners') sugar

1–2 teaspoons water

GINGER BISCUITS

METHOD

1 Preheat the oven to 180°C/350°F/Gas mark 6. Grease a baking tray with a little butter or oil, or line it with baking parchment.

2 Cream the butter and sugar together in a mixing bowl, then add the golden syrup and ground ginger and mix together well.

3 Add the flour and the bicarbonate of soda and mix.

4 Turn out the dough onto a well floured surface. Using a rolling pin, roll the dough out to about 3mm (⅛ inch) thick. Cut shapes out (see tip below). Keep them roughly the same size so that they cook evenly.

5 Lay the shapes on the prepared baking tray, leaving space between them as they will spread slightly in the oven.

6 Bake the biscuits for 10–12 minutes until golden brown. Carefully take the tray out of the oven with oven gloves. Leave the biscuits to cool slightly on the tray before lifting onto a wire rack to cool completely.

7 When the biscuits are cold, decorate them, if you wish. Mix the icing sugar and water together to create icing thick enough to pipe. Put the icing mixture into a piping bag with a small tip and pipe details onto your biscuits.

 This is a good basic recipe for making any shapes, from gingerbread people to Christmas tree decorations. If you are making decorations for your tree, make sure to cut a small hole into the top of the shape before baking so that you can thread a ribbon or piece of string through the biscuit.

Photographed with piped icing

Serves 8

 Suitable for freezing

 Electric hand mixer

Cut off a slice to serve, and keep the rest whole in an airtight container until serving.

INGREDIENTS

Butter or vegetable oil, for greasing

65g (2¼oz) butter or margarine

125g (4½oz) caster sugar

1 egg

1 very ripe banana

100g (3½oz) wholemeal flour (or plain white/all-purpose flour)

½ teaspoon bicarbonate of soda (baking soda)

40g (1½oz) chopped walnuts (optional)

BANANA BREAD

METHOD

1. Preheat the oven to 170°C/325°F/Gas mark 5 if you are making the banana bread in a loaf tin. (If you are making muffins, preheat the oven to 180°C/350°F/Gas mark 6.)

2. Grease a 450g (1lb) loaf tin (measuring about 20 x 10 x 6cm/8 x 4 x 2½ inch) and line it with baking parchment (or put 8 muffin cases into a muffin tin).

3. Put the butter or margarine into a mixing bowl. Make sure it is soft enough to mix easily. If it is not, put it into the microwave in a microwaveable bowl for 10–20 seconds to soften (but not melt!).

4. Add the caster sugar to the butter and beat together with a wooden spoon or electric hand mixer until creamy.

5. Crack the egg separately to make sure there is no shell in it, then add it to the bowl. Mix it in thoroughly.

6. Peel the banana, chop it into rough pieces and add them to the bowl.

7. Add the flour, bicarbonate of soda and nuts, if using, and mix in gently.

8. Pour the mixture into the loaf tin and bake in the oven for 35 minutes, or until it is firm to touch in the middle. Take it out of the oven and leave it to cool in the tin before turning the loaf cake out. (If you are making muffins, spoon the mixture evenly into 8 muffin cases, filling them three-quarters of the way up. Bake them in the oven for 20 minutes, until firm to touch.)

 This is a great recipe for using up bananas that have gone black and soft that not many people want to eat! Using wholemeal flour will increase the fibre content.

Photographed with walnuts

Makes 12 tarts

 Suitable for freezing

JAM TARTS

INGREDIENTS

Flour, for rolling out

1 x quantity shortcrust pastry (see page 178) or 250g (9oz) shop-bought shortcrust pastry

12 teaspoons strawberry, raspberry, apricot or blackcurrant jam (about 200g/7oz)

METHOD

1   Preheat the oven to 200°C/400°F/Gas mark 7.

2   Dust the work surface with flour, then roll out your pastry using a rolling pin until it is about 2mm (1/16 inch) thick.

3   Using a 9cm (3½ inch) round cutter, cut out 12 circles from your pastry. If you don't have a cutter, you can cut around something of a similar diameter, such as a glass or mug, using a knife. You may need to gather up the 'pastry scraps' and re-roll the pastry to make all 12 circles.

4   Place each pastry circle into a hole in your cupcake tray and press down gently.

5   Put a teaspoon of jam into the middle of each pastry case.

6   Bake them in the oven for 10 minutes, or until the pastry is golden brown.

7   Carefully take them out of the oven with oven gloves and leave them to cool slightly before removing them from the tray.

 You can use any flavoured jam, or try making them with sweet mincemeat at Christmas time.

Photographed with raspberry, blackcurrant and apricot jam

Makes 20 cookies

 Suitable for freezing

CHOCOLATE CHIP COOKIES

INGREDIENTS

Butter or vegetable oil,
  for greasing

150g (5½oz) butter

80g (2¾oz) granulated sugar

80g (2¾oz) demerara sugar

1 teaspoon vanilla extract

1 egg

220g (7¾oz) plain
  (all-purpose) flour

½ teaspoon bicarbonate of
  soda (baking soda)

Pinch of salt

200g (7oz) chocolate chips

METHOD

1   Preheat the oven to 180°C/350°F/Gas mark 6. Grease two baking trays with a little butter or oil, or line them with baking parchment. If you only have one baking tray, bake the cookies in two batches.

2   Put the butter into a mixing bowl. Make sure it is soft enough to mix easily. If it is not, put it into the microwave in a microwaveable bowl for 10–20 seconds to soften (but not melt!).

3   Add both the sugars to the butter and beat together with a wooden spoon until creamy.

4   Add the vanilla extract. Crack the egg separately in a mug or small bowl to make sure there is no shell in it, then add it to the bowl. Mix it in thoroughly.

5   Add the flour, bicarbonate of soda and salt and mix.

6   Add the chocolate chips and mix them in.

7   Use a teaspoon to pick up small scoops of mixture and place them on the baking trays, spacing them well apart to allow for spreading. The mixture should make about 20 cookies.

8   Bake the cookies for 10–15 minutes until lightly brown.

9   Leave them to cool on the baking tray for a couple of minutes, then carefully lift them onto a wire rack to cool completely.

  You can use white, milk or dark chocolate chips, or a combination! The different sugars add extra crunch, but if you don't have this type you can substitute them with 160g (5¾oz) caster sugar.

 Makes 12 cookies

 Suitable for freezing

OAT & GINGER COOKIES

INGREDIENTS

Butter or vegetable oil, for greasing

100g (3½oz) dried apricots

50g (1¾oz) stem ginger (about 4 balls)

50g (1¾oz) plain (all-purpose) flour

½ teaspoon bicarbonate of soda (baking soda)

225g (8oz) porridge oats

1 teaspoon ground cinnamon

80g (2¾oz) dried cranberries or sultanas (golden raisins)

150g (5½oz) butter

150g (5½oz) demerara sugar

100g (3½oz) golden syrup (light corn syrup)

1 egg

METHOD

1   Preheat the oven to 180°C/350°F/Gas mark 6. Grease two baking trays with a little butter or oil, or line them with baking parchment. If you only have one baking tray, bake the cookies in two batches.

2   Chop the apricots and ginger into small pieces.

3   Put the flour, bicarbonate of soda, oats, cinnamon, cranberries (or sultanas), chopped apricots and ginger into a mixing bowl and mix them together.

4   Melt the butter, sugar and golden syrup in a saucepan over a low heat (or melt them together in a microwaveable bowl or measuring jug in the microwave for about 40 seconds, until the butter is melted).

5   Pour the butter mixture into the mixing bowl and stir it all together.

6   Crack the egg into a cup and beat it with a fork, then add it to the mixture and stir in.

7   Place 6 heaped tablespoons of the mixture on each baking tray, allowing space for spreading during cooking.

8   Bake the cookies in the oven for 10–12 minutes. Carefully take them out of the oven with oven gloves and allow them to cool before removing them from the baking tray.

 This is a cake-type cookie so will be softer than a biscuit.

Makes 12 flapjacks

 Suitable for freezing

 HOW TO: MAKING A PIPING BAG

 HOW TO: PIPING CHOCOLATE

FLAPJACKS

INGREDIENTS

Butter or vegetable oil, for greasing

150g (5½oz) golden syrup (light corn syrup)

150g (5½oz) sugar

150g (5½oz) butter or margarine

300g (10½oz) rolled oats

100g (3½oz) dark (bittersweet) chocolate, to decorate (optional)

METHOD

1   Preheat the oven to 160°C/315°F/Gas mark 4. Grease a small rectangular tin (measuring about 26 x 20cm/10½ x 8 inch) or 12-hole cupcake tray with a little butter or oil, or line the tin with baking parchment.

2   Put the golden syrup, sugar and butter into a small microwaveable bowl and melt in the microwave for about 1 minute, or until the butter has melted.

3   Put the oats into a mixing bowl. Carefully pour the melted ingredients over the oats and mix them together well with a wooden spoon.

4   Tip the mixture into the tin, or divide it equally between the holes of a cupcake tray, and press the mixture down with the back of a spoon so you have an even layer.

5   Bake the flapjacks in the oven for 20 minutes until golden brown.

6   Remove the tray from the oven carefully, using oven gloves. If using the rectangular tin, carefully score the flapjacks into 12 squares with a sharp knife while the flapjacks are still hot.

7   Leave the flapjacks to cool and then remove them from the tin.

8   If you are decorating the flapjacks with chocolate, break the chocolate into small pieces and put them into a small microwaveable bowl or measuring jug. Heat the chocolate in the microwave for 20 seconds, then stir and return to the microwave for another 20 seconds. Repeat these steps until the chocolate is melted and runny. (Alternatively, melt the chocolate in a bowl over a pan of simmering water.) Pour the melted chocolate into a piping bag and drizzle it over the flapjacks.

 This recipe is for a plain flapjack, but you can add other ingredients such as chopped dried apricots or mango, or add 25g (1oz) desiccated coconut and reduce the oats to 275g (9¾oz).

Photographed with a drizzle of dark chocolate

Makes 8 scones

 Suitable for freezing

SCONES

HOW TO:

RUBBING IN
METHOD

INGREDIENTS

Butter or vegetable oil,
for greasing

250g (9oz) self-raising flour,
plus extra for dusting

40g (1½oz) butter or
margarine

75g (2½oz) grated Cheddar
cheese and ½ teaspoon
mustard, OR
75g (2½oz) sultanas
(golden raisins) and
1 teaspoon ground
spice, such as cinnamon
(optional)

125ml (4fl oz) milk, plus extra
for glazing

Serve sweet
scones with
clotted or whipped
cream and jam
and cheese
scones with cream
cheese.

METHOD

1   Preheat the oven to 210°C/415°F/Gas mark 8. Grease a baking tray
with a little butter or oil.

2   Put the flour into a bowl. Add the butter and rub it into the flour
with your fingertips.

3   If adding optional flavourings to the scones, add either the grated
cheese and mustard or the sultanas and spice. Mix the ingredients
together.

4   Pour the milk in and mix it through with a palette knife (or butter
knife). Using one hand only, mix the dough until it all comes
together.

5   Lightly dust the work surface with flour and roll out the dough to a
thickness of 2cm (¾ inch). Using a 7cm (2¾ inch) diameter round
cutter, cut out 8 circles from the dough and place them on the
baking tray, leaving space in between. If you don't have cutters,
divide the dough into 8 equal pieces and roll them into balls with
your hands, then flatten them slightly on the tray.

6   Brush each scone with a little bit of milk to create a glaze. Bake
them in the oven for 8–12 minutes, until lightly golden brown.

7   Leave to cool on a wire rack.

✺   If you aren't freezing them, these scones need to be
eaten fresh on the day they are made as there is not
much fat in them, so they will go stale quickly.

Photographed with whipped cream and strawberry jam

ICED BISCUITS

HOW TO:

MAKING A PIPING BAG

HOW TO:

PIPING & FLOODING BISCUITS

INGREDIENTS

Butter or vegetable oil, for greasing

100g (3½oz) butter or block margarine

100g (3½oz) caster sugar

1 egg

200g (7oz) plain (all-purpose) flour, plus extra for dusting

For the icing

200g (7oz) icing (confectioners') sugar

1–2 tablespoons water

Food colouring (optional)

METHOD

1 Preheat the oven to 180°C/350°F/Gas mark 6. Grease a baking tray with a little butter or oil.

2 Put the butter or margarine into a mixing bowl. Make sure it is soft enough to mix easily. If it is not, put it into the microwave in a microwaveable bowl for 10–20 seconds to soften (but not melt!).

3 Add the caster sugar to the butter and beat together with a wooden spoon until creamy.

4 Crack the egg into a cup and beat it lightly with a fork. Add the egg to the mixing bowl and beat the mixture with a tablespoon of the flour.

5 Add the rest of the flour to the bowl and mix it together to form a soft dough.

6 Dust a work surface lightly with flour and turn out the dough. Using a rolling pin, roll out the dough until it is about 5mm (¼ inch) thick.

7 Cut the biscuits into shapes, either with a knife or a cookie cutter. Keep the biscuits roughly the same size so that they cook evenly. Place them on the baking tray with a bit of space between each biscuit as they will spread in the oven.

8 Bake for 10–12 minutes, until light golden in colour. Carefully take the tray out of the oven with oven gloves. Leave the biscuits to cool on the tray slightly before lifting onto a wire rack to cool completely and harden.

9 When the biscuits are cold, decorate them. Mix the icing sugar and water together to create icing thick enough to pipe. Put half of the icing mixture into a piping bag and pipe an outline onto each biscuit. Add a teaspoon more water to the remaining icing to make it runnier and mix in food colouring of your choice. Use the icing to flood the inner portion of the biscuit.

Serves 12

 Suitable for freezing

 Electric hand mixer

HOW TO:

TURNING OUT CAKES

INGREDIENTS

Butter or vegetable oil, for greasing

200g (7oz) butter or margarine

200g (7oz) caster sugar

1 teaspoon vanilla extract

4 eggs

200g (7oz) self-raising flour

SPONGE CAKE
(OR CUPCAKES)

METHOD

1 Preheat the oven to 180°C/350°F/Gas mark 6. Grease two 20cm (8 inch) round cake tins with a little butter or oil and line the bottom of each tin with a circle of baking parchment. (Or place 24 cupcake cases into cupcake tins.)

2 Put the butter or margarine into a mixing bowl. Make sure it is soft enough to mix easily. If it is not, put it into the microwave in a microwaveable bowl for 10–20 seconds to soften (but not melt!).

3 Cream together the butter and sugar with a wooden spoon or an electric hand mixer.

4 Add the vanilla extract. Crack the eggs separately into a small bowl to make sure there is no shell in them, then add them to the bowl. Mix thoroughly.

5 Carefully mix in the flour with a metal spoon. Try not to beat it too hard as this knocks the air out of the mixture, making your cake dense.

6 Pour half the mixture into each cake tin and spread it out evenly (or spoon the mixture evenly into the cupcake cases).

7 Bake the cakes in the oven for 25–30 minutes until golden brown (or bake the cupcakes for 15 minutes).

8 Carefully remove the cakes from the oven with oven gloves. Turn them out onto a wire rack and leave them to cool (or leave the cupcakes to cool in the paper cases on a wire rack).

 Once completely cold, sandwich the cakes together with jam and whipped cream or butter icing to make a Victoria sandwich cake. For cupcakes, ice them with butter icing (see page 180).

Photographed sandwiched together with butter icing and jam, with a dusting of icing (confectioners') sugar on top

Serves 12

 Suitable for freezing

 Electric hand mixer

HOW TO:

TURNING
OUT CAKES

INGREDIENTS

For the cake

Butter or vegetable oil,
for greasing

250g (9oz) caster sugar

100g (3½oz) soft brown sugar

400g (14oz) plain (all-
purpose) flour

1 teaspoon bicarbonate of
soda (baking soda)

2 teaspoons baking powder

50g (1¾oz) cocoa powder

180g (6¼oz) butter

130ml (4fl oz) vegetable oil

300ml (10½fl oz) cold water

3 large eggs

150ml (5fl oz) sour cream

1 tablespoon vanilla extract

For the icing

200g (7oz) dark (bittersweet)
chocolate

250g (9oz) butter

300g (10½oz) icing
(confectioners') sugar

1 teaspoon vanilla extract

CHOCOLATE CAKE

METHOD

1 Preheat the oven to 170°C/325°F/Gas mark 5. Grease two 20cm (8 inch) round cake tins with a little butter or oil and then line them with baking parchment.

2 In a large mixing bowl, put both sugars, flour, bicarbonate of soda, baking powder and cocoa, and mix them all together with a wooden spoon.

3 Melt the butter in a microwaveable bowl in the microwave for approximately 1 minute or in a saucepan over a low heat.

4 Add the oil to the butter and beat them together with an electric hand mixer. Add the cold water and mix it in. Add this to the dry ingredients and beat it in using the electric hand mixer (or wooden spoon).

5 Add the eggs to the mixture one at a time (crack separately in a cup to check there is no shell before adding) and mix together. Add the sour cream and vanilla extract and mix them in.

6 Pour half the mixture into each cake tin and spread the mixture out evenly. Cook in the oven for 50 minutes, until firm to the touch. Remove the cakes from the oven carefully, using oven gloves, and leave to cool completely.

7 To make the icing, melt the chocolate in a small microwaveable bowl in the microwave, stirring every 20 seconds until smooth and melted. In a large bowl beat the butter with an electric mixer until it is soft. Sieve in the icing sugar and mix it through. Add the vanilla extract and chocolate and mix it together until it is smooth and glossy. Sandwich the 2 cakes together with a quarter of the icing and then spread the rest, to cover the top and sides of the cake.

 This takes longer than 1 hour if you are making the large cake and icing it. Alternatively, you can make 12 cupcakes by halving the quantity (use 2 small eggs). Put 12 muffin cases into a tin and fill two-thirds of the way up. Cook for 25 minutes.

BASICS

SALAD DRESSING/ VINAIGRETTE

INGREDIENTS

90ml (6 tablespoons) olive oil

2 tablespoons red or white wine vinegar, or lemon juice

Salt and pepper

Any combination of the following (all optional):

1 tablespoon honey or 1 teaspoon caster sugar

1 teaspoon mayonnaise

1 teaspoon mustard

1 teaspoon chopped herbs (such as parsley or tarragon)

1 large sprig rosemary or thyme to infuse into oil

1 garlic clove, thinly sliced

1 chilli, finely chopped

Lemon zest/peel strips

METHOD

1   Put all the ingredients into an old, clean jam jar. Put the lid on and shake it vigorously. If you don't have a jar, then put the ingredients into a jug and mix the dressing with a fork.

2   Taste for flavour and add salt and pepper to season.

 This can be kept in the fridge for up to 3 weeks, but remove from the fridge 30 minutes before using so that it can warm up and the oil is liquid. If it 'separates' out, just shake it again to combine all the ingredients before use. There are many different oils and vinegars that you can buy, so try different ones to change the flavour.

Left-hand bottle – lemon peel and thyme; middle bottle – garlic and rosemary; right-hand bottle – simple oil and vinegar

 Suitable for freezing

TOMATO SAUCE

INGREDIENTS

1 onion

1 garlic clove

1 tablespoon oil

1 x 400g (14oz) can of
   chopped tomatoes

Salt and pepper

1 teaspoon dried mixed herbs
   or 1 tablespoon chopped
   fresh herbs (such as basil
   or parsley)

Optional extras

1 red (bell) pepper

1 carrot

1 courgette (zucchini)

1 stick celery

50g (1¾oz) mushrooms

METHOD

1   Peel and chop the onion. Peel and crush or finely chop the garlic.

2   Prepare any other optional ingredients: cut the pepper in half, deseed and chop it into small pieces; peel and grate the carrot; cut the ends off the courgette and chop it into small pieces; chop the celery into small pieces; slice the mushrooms.

3   Heat the oil, onion and garlic in a saucepan on a medium heat. Cook them for about 5 minutes until they are soft, but not golden, stirring frequently.

4   Add the optional ingredient(s), and cook for a further 5 minutes, stirring occasionally until they are soft.

5   Add the tomatoes and a pinch of salt and pepper. Allow the sauce to simmer on a low heat for 10 minutes, stirring occasionally, until the sauce thickens slightly and becomes richer in flavour.

6   Add the herbs and stir through.

 This sauce can be used on pasta, in a lasagne or poured over fish and cooked in the oven.

WHITE SAUCE
(BÉCHAMEL)

INGREDIENTS

100g (3½oz) hard cheese, such as Cheddar (optional)

25g (1oz) plain (all-purpose) flour

25g (1oz) butter or margarine

575ml (20fl oz) milk

Black pepper

METHOD

1   Grate the cheese, if using.

2   Put the flour, butter and milk into a saucepan. Stir continuously with a whisk over a medium heat until all the lumps are gone and it turns into a smooth sauce. This will take about 5 minutes and the sauce will thicken once it starts to boil at the edges of the pan.

3   Once the sauce is thickening, stir it with a wooden spoon for 30 seconds. The sauce should coat the back of a wooden spoon when the correct consistency. Remove from the heat and add a pinch of black pepper.

4   Add the grated cheese immediately, if using, and stir in until it is melted.

 This recipe can be used in a lasagne, poured over fish and cooked in the oven, or on pasta with other ingredients such as cooked bacon or chopped fresh parsley. It is also used in the Vegetables in a Cheese Sauce recipe (see page 58).

Serves 4

 Suitable for freezing

 Saucepan with lid

Serve as a side dish to a main meal, or use in other recipes such as Shepherd's Pie (see page 70) or Fish Cakes (page 86).

INGREDIENTS

1kg (2lb 4 oz) potatoes

25g (1oz) butter

3–4 tablespoons milk

Salt and pepper

MASHED POTATO

METHOD

1   Boil a kettle full of water.

2   Peel and wash the potatoes and cut them into even-sized pieces (approximately 3 x 3cm/1¼ x 1¼ inch). Place them into a saucepan that has a lid. Pour boiling water over the potatoes until they are covered. Bring them to the boil and, once boiling, turn down the heat to low and simmer. Put the saucepan lid on and leave them to cook for about 20 minutes until they are soft.

3   Drain the potatoes in a colander or sieve over the sink. Tip the potatoes back into the saucepan.

4   Add the butter and milk and mash them together using a potato masher (or fork) until smooth.

5   Add salt and pepper to taste.

 To test if the potatoes are cooked, prod one with a fork or knife – it should easily go into the middle of the potato. If they are still hard in the middle, cook for a further 5 minutes and test again. You can also jazz it up a bit by adding 2 tablespoons of grated Cheddar, 1 tablespoon of wholegrain mustard, or 2 finely chopped spring onions (scallions).

Makes about 500g
(1lb 2oz)

 Suitable for freezing

This pastry can be used to make many dishes, including Sausage Rolls (see page 38) and Fruit Tarts (see page 126).

INGREDIENTS

200g (7oz) strong white flour, plus extra for dusting

Pinch of salt

150g (5½oz) butter or block margarine

130ml (4½fl oz) ice cold water

1 teaspoon lemon juice (optional)

ROUGH PUFF PASTRY

METHOD

1 Put the flour and salt in a mixing bowl.

2 Cut the butter into 1cm (½ inch) cubes and lightly mix them into the flour without rubbing in.

3 Measure the water in a measuring jug. Add the lemon juice to the water, if using.

4 Make a well in the centre of the dry ingredients and add the water. Stir with a butter knife to make a fairly stiff dough. Wrap the dough in cling film (plastic wrap) and place it in the fridge for 10 minutes to chill.

5 Turn the dough out onto a floured surface and roll it into a rectangle measuring about 30 x 10cm (12 x 4 inch), keeping the sides as straight as you can.

6 With a short edge in front of you, fold the bottom third of the rectangle up over the middle of the pastry sheet. Now fold the top third over to cover that.

7 Turn the pastry 90 degrees and roll it out again, repeating step 5 and 6 three more times. This creates layers of trapped air making your pastry rise and puff up once cooked.

8 Wrap the pastry in cling film and store it in the fridge until it is ready to be used.

 You can use a combination of fats (such as lard, butter, block margarine) as long as the total weight remains 150g (5½oz). The lemon juice makes the pastry slightly easier to work with as it won't shrink so much, plus it stops it going a grey colour.

Makes about 250g (9oz)

 Suitable for freezing

HOW TO:

RUBBING IN METHOD

SHORTCRUST PASTRY

INGREDIENTS

75g (2½oz) butter or block margarine

150g (5½oz) plain (all-purpose) flour, plus extra for dusting

2–4 tablespoons cold water

This pastry can be used to make lots of recipes, including Quiche (see page 92) or Jam Tarts (see page 150).

METHOD

1   Put the butter into a mixing bowl and cut it into small pieces using a butter knife.

2   Add the flour to the bowl and rub the butter into the flour using your fingertips, until it looks like breadcrumbs and there are no lumps remaining. Shake the bowl gently and the larger lumps will come to the surface, if there are any.

3   Add 2 tablespoons of cold water to the mixture and mix it together using a butter knife. Add more water, 1 tablespoon at a time, if the mixture does not stick together.

4   Use your hands to form the dough into a ball. Wrap it tightly in cling film (plastic wrap) and store it in the fridge until you are ready to use it.

Sandwiches and covers the top of a 20cm (8 inch) sponge, or 12 cupcakes

 Suitable for freezing

 Electric hand mixer (optional)

INGREDIENTS

100g (3½oz) butter or margarine, softened

300g (10½oz) icing (confectioners') sugar

2 tablespoons water (or a flavouring – see below)

A few drops of food colouring (optional)

BUTTER ICING

METHOD

1 Put the butter into a mixing bowl. Make sure the butter is soft enough to mix easily. If it is not, then put it into the microwave in a microwaveable bowl for 10–20 seconds to soften (but not melt!).

2 Sift the icing sugar into the bowl and mix it gently with an electric mixer (start slowly so that the icing sugar doesn't go everywhere) or with a wooden spoon until smooth.

3 Add the water and mix to the required consistency or add a flavouring.

4 For the optional flavourings, leave out the water and add one of the following:

Chocolate
Mix 3 tablespoons of cocoa powder with 2 tablespoons of hot water in a cup, then add to the icing sugar and butter mixture.

Lemon or orange
Add the juice and finely grated zest of a lemon or an orange to the icing sugar and butter mixture.

Coffee
Mix 2 heaped teaspoons of instant coffee with 2 tablespoons of boiling water in a cup and stir until dissolved before adding to the icing sugar and butter mixture.

 If the icing is too thick, add 1 tablespoon of water. If you have added too much liquid, add more icing sugar, 1 tablespoon at a time. The mixture should be thick enough to hold its shape but soft enough to spread. You can add various piping nozzles to your piping bag if using the icing to pipe patterns.

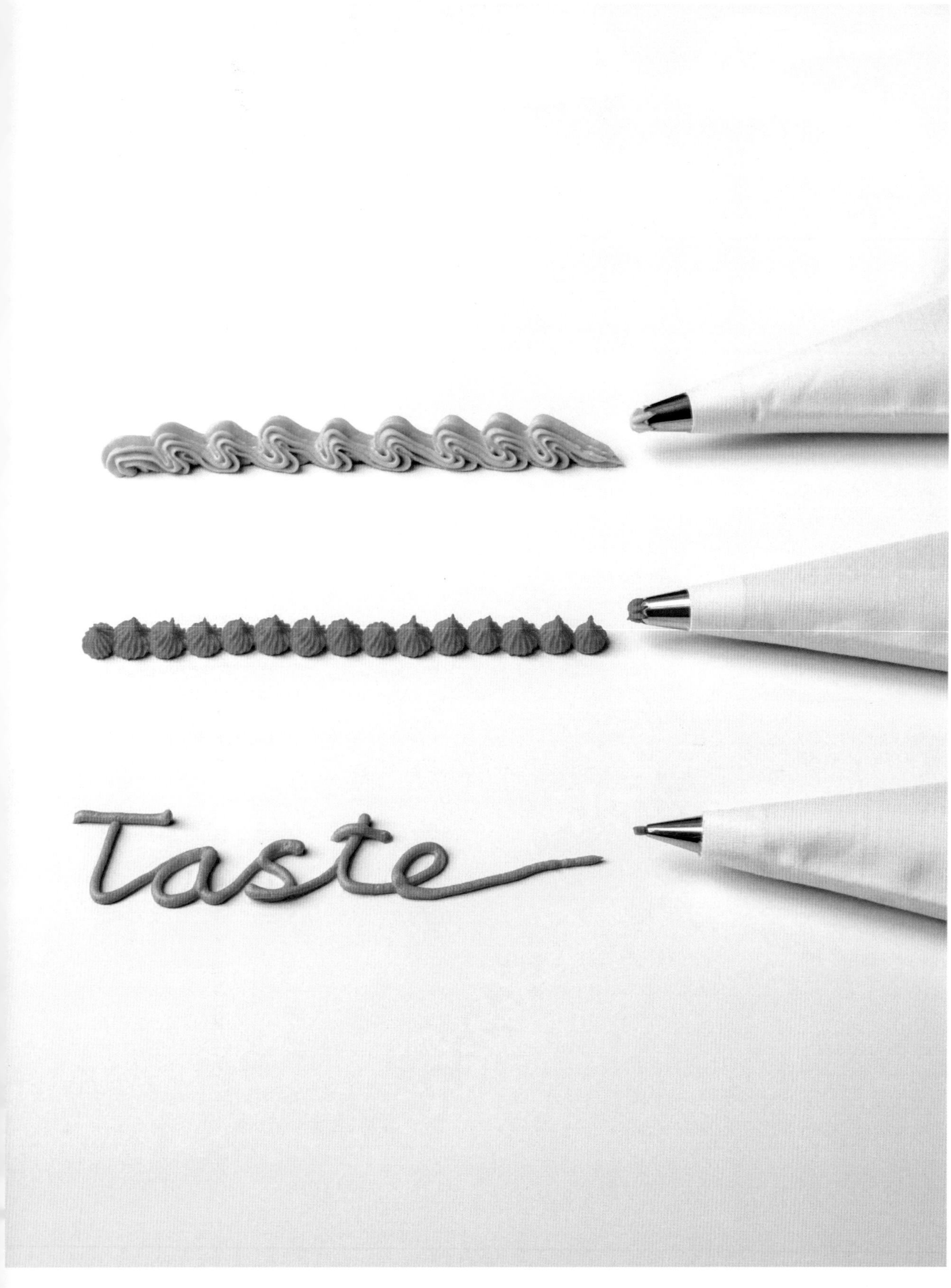
Taste

QR CODES
TUTORIAL VIDEO CLIPS

To access the videos, open the camera app on your phone, then focus the camera on the QR code by tapping the code. Follow the instructions on the screen to open the tutorial video. All video clips can be found at www.sarahmaincooks.com/cooking-tips

BAKING BLIND
Quiche (page 92)
Bakewell Tart (page 122)

LINING A FLAN TIN WITH PASTRY
Quiche (page 92)
Lemon Meringue Pie
    (page 114)
Bakewell Tart (page 122)

FOLDING SAMOSAS
Samosas (page 44)

MAKING A PIPING BAG
Ginger Biscuits (page 146)
Flapjacks (page 156)
Iced Biscuits (page 160)

HALVE AND STONE AN AVOCADO
Guacamole (page 30)
Fajitas (page 76)

MAKING AN APPLE STRUDEL
Apple Strudel (page 118)

KNEADING DOUGH
Naan Bread (page 46)
Bread Rolls (page 48)

MAKING CROUTONS
Carrot & Coriander Soup
    (page 18)

PEELING AND CORING APPLES
Fruit Crumble (page 116)
Apple Strudel (page 118)
Apple, Blueberry &
    Cinnamon Muffins
    (page 144)

SEPARATING EGGS
Lemon Meringue Pie
    (page 114)
Vanilla & Almond Biscuits
    (page 136)

PIPING AND FLOODING BISCUITS
Iced Biscuits (page 160)

SHAPING SPRING ROLLS
Spring Rolls (page 50)

PIPING CHOCOLATE
Flapjacks (page 156)

SKINNING TOMATOES
Tomato Soup (page 20)

RUBBING IN METHOD
Fruit Crumble (page 116)
Shortbread Biscuits
    (page 134)
Scones (page 158)
Shortcrust pastry (page 178)

TURNING OUT CAKES
Pineapple Upside Down
    Cake (page 128)
Carrot Cake (page 138)
Almond Cake (page 142)
Sponge Cake (page 162)
Chocolate Cake (page 164)

SEALING AND CRIMPING
Sausage Rolls (page 38)
Cornish Pasties (page 42)

GLOSSARY

Baking blind – the process of cooking a pastry case in the oven, either partially or completely, without a filling. To do this, you roll out the pastry and place it in a tin with baking parchment over the top. You then place ceramic baking beans (or rice) all over the pastry case to weigh it down, before cooking it in the oven. Make sure all baking beans/rice and baking parchment are removed after baking blind, before filling the pastry case.

Basting – scooping up the juices/sauce from a pan with a spoon and tipping back over the food being cooked. This process keeps the food moist and succulent.

Batter – this is usually a mixture that is runny, containing flour, egg and a liquid. Pancake mixture is a good example of a batter.

Boiling – this is when liquid in a saucepan on a high heat produces rapid, big bubbles.

Caramelisation – this term is used when heating sugar until it melts, turning it brown and changing its flavour. This can be done in a saucepan to create caramel or spun sugar, or the sugar can simply be grilled or blow torched on the top of a crème brûlée, for example. The term is also used to describe the process of frying onions to a dark golden colour, making them sweeter.

Crimping – used to join two pieces of pastry by pinching together (or pressing with the tines of a fork) to seal them, and create a decorative effect on the edge.

Deseeding – removing the seeds from fruit or vegetables, such as peppers or chillies.

Folding in – gently mixing ingredients by carefully lifting the mixture from the bottom using a metal spoon or spatula and turning it over as you bring it to the top until all the ingredients are gently combined. This method is used when you need your mixture to remain light and airy.

Grating – the process of shredding food into smaller pieces. This can be done by using a grater, which usually has various sized, sharp-bladed holes on it. The larger holes can be used for ingredients such as hard cheeses or carrots, while the smaller holes can be used, for example, to zest citrus fruit.

Greasing – using a pastry brush or small piece of baking parchment to spread oil or butter evenly over a tray, cake tin or dish to stop food sticking during cooking.

Kneading – the process of mixing and stretching a dough to evenly distribute the ingredients and to make the mixture smooth, particularly when making bread. It can be done by hand or using a machine with a dough hook.

Laminating – this is the term used when creating layers in puff pastry by rolling it out and folding it over itself several times. Lamination traps air so that, when the pastry is cooked, it rises up to create crispy layers.

Reducing – this term refers to the thickening or concentrating of liquids, which in turn creates a stronger flavour. This is usually applied to sauces, stews, stocks and soups.

Rubbing in – the technique of coating a fat such as butter or margarine in flour, using your fingertips and thumbs, to create a breadcrumb-like texture. You can also do this using a food processor.

Scoring – making a cut/slit in the top of something, usually pastry or fatty meat.

Separating eggs – the process where the egg yolk and the egg white are split apart. It is essential that the two are not mixed together for some recipes where just the white is needed to create a foam, such as meringues or soufflés.

Simmering – this is when liquid in a saucepan bubbles with tiny bubbles, just below boiling. Often you bring something to the boil first, then lower the heat to 'simmer'.

Skinning tomatoes – removing the skin of tomatoes by carefully making a cross through the base of their skin (and not into the flesh of the tomato) using a sharp knife, then plunging them into a bowl of boiling water for 1 minute, removing to cool slightly, and then peeling off the skin.

Zesting – removing the thin, outer skin (the coloured part) of citrus fruits such as lemons and limes, by peeling or grating them finely.

INDEX

CONVERSION CHARTS

WEIGHT

20g	¾oz
25g	1oz
50g	1¾oz
75g	2½oz
100g	3½oz
125g	4½oz
150g	5½oz
175g	6oz
200g	7oz
225g	8oz
250g	9oz
275g	9¾oz
300g	10½oz
350g	12oz
400g	14oz
450g	1lb
500g	1lb 2oz
550g	1lb 3oz
600g	1lb 5oz
650g	1lb 7oz
700g	1lb 9oz
750g	1lb 10oz
1kg	2lb 2oz

TEMPERATURE

120°C / 250°F / Gas mark 1
140°C / 275°F / Gas mark 2
150°C / 300°F / Gas mark 3
160°C / 315°F / Gas mark 4
170°C / 325°F / Gas mark 5
180°C / 350°F / Gas mark 6
190°C / 375°F / Gas mark 6
200°C / 400°F / Gas mark 7
210°C / 415°F / Gas mark 8
220°C / 425°F / Gas mark 8

VOLUME

50ml	1¾fl oz
100ml	3½fl oz
120ml	4fl oz
150ml	5¼fl oz
200ml	6¾fl oz
250ml	9fl oz
300ml	10fl oz
400ml	14fl oz
500ml	17fl oz
600ml	20¼fl oz
700ml	24fl oz
800ml	27fl oz
900ml	30½fl oz
1l	35fl oz

SIZE

3mm (⅛ inch)
1cm (½ inch)
2cm (¾ inch)
3cm (1⅛ inch)
4cm (1½ inch)
5cm (2 inch)
7cm (2¾ inch)
8cm (3 inch)
9cm (3½ inch)
10cm (4 inch)
20cm (8 inch)
22cm (8½ inch)
30cm (12 inch)
40cm (16 inch)
50cm (20 inch)

ACKNOWLEDGEMENTS

Thank you to my Mum, who has always been a great cook, making sure we always had at least one green vegetable on our plate at every meal and making her chicken pies, paella and steamed syrup puddings for us. She encouraged me to cook as a teenager and lots of the recipes in this book originated from her.

Thank you to Elspeth for trialling lots of the recipes, photographing initial ideas and setting up the format of the book as well as creating the sushi photo for the book. Thank you to Katie, who has a keen eye for detail, particularly editing the book and checking my appalling grammar and spelling, standardising everything, checking ingredients are in the right order, and for her spicy rice, for which she created the recipe and took the photo. She has spent days checking, re-checking and commenting on the recipes – being extremely thorough and making me laugh. She continues to help me now with Instagram. Thanks to Harry for eating the trials (particularly the sausage rolls) and to Rosie for her social media advice. Thank you to David for cycling food around to Christine and bringing me cups of tea while I worked.

Thank you to Christine Bradshaw, who is an amazing photographer and perfectionist. I never knew how much time and effort went into one photo! Thank you to all those who have lent props for the photographs, too.

Thank you to Chris Hall, who did the graphic design work and shaped the book's first draft. Thank you to Jamie Thorn, who created the video clip tutorials for the QR codes and got me started on Instagram.

Thank you to Kate Millar for being my best friend since Catering College, and for all her support.

Thank you to Alison Price for introducing me to Michael Watts, and to Michael for introducing me, in turn, to Polly Powell and all those at Batsford Books, for publishing the book.

ABOUT THE AUTHOR

Sarah Main has been a teacher of Food, Textiles and Design Technology for over 30 years, and has taught thousands of children how to cook. Sarah first trained in Catering and Hotel Management and then went on to achieve a Bachelor of Education Honours degree. *The Independent Cook* is her first book. She lives in West London.

First published in the United Kingdom
in 2024 by
Batsford
43 Great Ormond Street
London
WC1N 3HZ

An imprint of B. T. Batsford Holdings Limited

ISBN 978 1 84994 936 1

A CIP catalogue record for this book is available from the British Library.

10 9 8 7 6 5 4 3 2 1

Reproduction by Rival Colour Ltd, UK
Printed in Turkey by Elma Basim

This book can be ordered direct from the publisher at
www.batsfordbooks.com, or try your local bookshop.

MIX
From well-
managed forests
FSC
www.fsc.org   FSC® C164814